BEER *and* SPIRITS

A Guide to Haunted Pubs
in the Black Country
& Surrounding Area

DAVID TAYLOR AND ANDREW HOMER

FOREWORD BY INTERNATIONAL GHOST HUNTER
PETER UNDERWOOD

AMBERLEY

David Taylor
To my wife Carolyn, for everything.

Andrew Homer
To my daughter Sophie, for just being herself.

First published 2010

Amberley Publishing plc
Cirencester Road, Chalford,
Stroud, Gloucestershire, GL6 8PE

www.amberley-books.com

British Library Cataloguing in Publication Data.
A catalogue record for this book is available from the British Library.

ISBN 978-1-84868-266-5

Typeset in 10pt on 12pt Sabon.
Typesetting and Origination by Amberley Publishing.
Printed in the UK.

Contents

Foreword

It gives me great pleasure to contribute briefly to this excellent and absorbing labour of love devoted to the many fascinating pubs of the Black County, their ghosts and their wares.

Public houses are a microcosm of human nature and as a setting for human drama they are without equal. Pubs have seen it all: love and laughter, happiness and unhappiness, pity, anger, grief, solitude, gaiety and the rest. Is it any wonder that some of these poignant and deeply felt emotions have, under certain conditions and perhaps in the presence of certain people, become somehow imprinted or impressed forever on the atmosphere and, again under certain conditions and perhaps in the presence of certain people, are replayed almost like a gramophone record? It may be a question of being in the right place at the right time to witness such psychic activity.

It is a certain fact that over recent decades inns and pubs have changed landlords, become incorporated into large chains, lost their character or closed completely, and consequently and lamentably the old stories and experiences are quickly forgotten and would be lost forever – were it not for such books as this. I wish it every success which it richly deserves.

Peter Underwood

Savage Club
1 Whitehall Place
London SW1A 2HD

Peter Underwood FRSA is the author of forty-six books on ghosts and other subjects, is a veteran television broadcaster and internationally renowned paranormal investigator. He is President of the Ghost Club Society and the Unitarian Society for Psychical Studies.

About the Authors

David Taylor

David is Chairman of Parasearch which he founded in 1986 to investigate paranormal phenomena in the Midlands. He is on the editorial board of the Association for the Scientific Study of Anomalous Phenomena (ASSAP) for which he is also an approved investigator. In 2009, he was presented with the Michael Bentine Memorial Award by ASSAP for his investigations. David is also Central England Regional Co-ordinator for The Ghost Club, founded in 1862, making it the oldest paranormal research group in the world. He is also editor of the Unitarian Society for Psychical Studies journal. He is also member of the Society for Psychical Research and The Churches Fellowship for Psychical & Spiritual Studies. Along with members of Parasearch he has spent countless nights in a variety of haunted locations around the country. David has appeared on television and radio relating to the paranormal and has lectured to a variety of organisations including the National Trust, The Architecture Centre, The Folklore Society, ASSAP, The Ghost Club and various national charities on many aspects of parapsychology, folklore and history. He is co-author of one book of ghosts (with Anne Bradford) and has had his research published in various magazines and journals. David is a professional graphic designer who runs Parasearch with his wife, Carolyn.

On the rare occasions when he is not investigating anomalous experiences or writing, he can be found in the company of his cat Felicity, or in old churches or second-hand bookshops.

David Taylor can be contacted at: david.taylor@parasearch.org.uk.

Andrew Homer

Andrew is joint national investigations co-ordinator for the Association for the Scientific Study of Anomalous Phenomena (ASSAP) and is a past Vice Chairman of West Midlands paranormal research group, Parasearch. He is a previous winner of the Michael Bentine Memorial Award for anomaly research carried out in a local retirement home. Andrew has contributed to many publications over the years and has presented lectures for the FT Unconvention, ASSAP and the Ghost Club. Currently an ASSAP executive committee member, he is also managing editor for the ASSAP journal, *Anomaly*. He has taken part in many notable investigations over years of anomaly research with both Parasearch and ASSAP and has appeared on numerous radio and television programmes. Andrew has investigated alleged anomalous phenomena in every type of location including castles, stately homes, private houses and, of course, public houses.

Appropriately enough, when he is not involved in anomaly research or writing, Andrew enjoys a pint in a real ale pub – haunted of course!

Andrew Homer can be contacted at: assapinvestigations@assap.org.

Acknowledgements

When we began to write this book back in 1996, neither of us thought that it would take us this long to finish it. This book would not have been possible without the generous help of the landlords, staff and customers of all the pubs listed and all the members of Parasearch, past and present for their valuable assistance on vigils in the pubs mentioned. We are grateful to Peter Underwood, one of the foremost authors and researchers on the subject of ghosts for agreeing to write the foreword. We are also grateful for the encouragement of Guy Lyon Playfair and the late Andrew Green, and for their permission to quote from their books. A big thank you must also go to Ken Taylor and Steve Potter for supplying photographs of pubs in Wordsley and Tipton and to Sophie Homer for the phantom hitchhiker artwork and the late Stan Hill for all his help with this project.

Introduction

By Andrew Homer & David Taylor

Of Beer ...

What is it about the British and their pubs? They are places that generate strong feelings, almost in the same way that football teams do. Whatever your opinion of them, one thing you have to agree on – they are an important aspect of our social history. In 1909, one pedestrian walking a half-mile stretch of road between Brierley Hill and Dudley, counted three public houses every minute, and there were five of them at Five Ways, Brierley Hill. A check of Kelly's Directories for 1928 showed some 1,500 public houses in the Black Country!

The people of these isles have been drinking ale since the Bronze Age. However, it was the arrival of the Romans and the establishment of the Roman road network that the first Inns called tabernae, in which the traveller could obtain refreshment, began to appear. When the Romans finally left, the Anglo-Saxons established alehouses that grew out of domestic dwellings. These alehouses formed meeting houses for the locals to meet and gossip and arrange mutual help within their communities. Here lies the beginning of the modern pub. They became so commonplace that in 965 King Edgar decreed that there should be no more than one alehouse per village.

A traveller in the early Middle Ages could obtain overnight accommodation in monasteries, but later a demand for hostelries grew with the popularity of pilgrimages and travel. In our own region, on the slopes of the Clent Hills the popular shrine of St Kenelm drew so many pilgrims that a pub, The Sign of the Red Cow, was established to quench the thirst of weary travellers.

Traditional English ale was made solely from fermented malt. The practice of adding hops to produce beer was introduced from the Netherlands in the early fifteenth century. Alehouses would each brew their own distinctive ale, but independent breweries began to appear in the late seventeenth century. By the end of the century almost all beer was brewed by commercial breweries.

The eighteenth century saw a huge growth in the number of drinking establishments, primarily due to the introduction of gin. Gin was brought to England by the Dutch after the Glorious Revolution of 1688 and started to become very popular after the government created a market for grain that was unfit to be used in brewing by allowing unlicensed gin production, while imposing a heavy duty on all imported spirits. As thousands of gin-shops sprang up all over England, brewers fought back by increasing the number of alehouses. By 1740 the production of gin had increased to six times that of beer and because of its cheapness it became popular with the poor, leading to the so-called Gin Craze. Over half of the 15,000 drinking establishments in London were gin-shops.

Many of the pubs in this book owe their very existence to gin-shops and one of our most famous military leaders, Arthur Wellesley. Later to become Duke of Wellington, he commanded the army that defeated Napoleon at the battle of Waterloo. Wellington returned to politics after the Napoleonic wars becoming Prime Minister in 1828. In 1830, his government introduced the Beerhouse Act. This was intended to replace the notorious gin-shops of the day by removing the tax on a healthier alternative – beer.

The act enabled virtually any house or shop owner to create a 'public house' on payment of two guineas to the local magistrates. This created a plethora of small beer houses both brewing and selling beer. In the Black Country, it was common for shops to set aside a room for the sale and consumption of beer. In this book you will discover examples of Black Country pubs which, prior to the 1830 Beerhouse Act started out as butcher's shops of all things!

The Sign of a Good Beer!

Traditional pubs are truly works of art. Sadly today, along with the more traditional pub names, they may be becoming a thing of the past. This is a great shame, for both are examples of how pubs connect us with social history.

In 1393, King Richard II compelled landlords to erect signs outside their premises. The legislation stated, 'Whosoever shall brew ale in the town with intention of selling it must hang out a sign, otherwise he shall forfeit his ale.' This was in order to make them easily visible to passing inspectors, borough ale tasters, who would decide the quality of the ale they provided. William Shakespeare's father, John Shakespeare, was one such inspector.

Another important factor was that during the Middle Ages a large percentage of the population would have been illiterate and so pictures on a sign were more useful than words as a means of identifying a public house. For this reason there was often no reason to write the establishment's name on the sign and inns opened without a formal written name, the name being derived later from the illustration on the sign.

The earliest signs were often not painted but consisted, for example, of paraphernalia connected with the brewing process such as bunches of hops or brewing implements, which were suspended above the door of the public house. In some cases local nicknames, farming terms and puns were also used. Local events were also often commemorated in pub signs. Simple natural or religious symbols such as the 'The Sun', 'The Star' and 'The Cross' were also incorporated into pub signs, sometimes being adapted to incorporate elements of the heraldry (e.g. the coat of arms) of the local lords who owned the lands upon which the public house stood. Some pubs also have Latin inscriptions.

Other subjects that lent themselves to visual depiction included the name of battles (e.g. Trafalgar), explorers, local notables, discoveries, sporting heroes and members of the royal family. Some pub signs are in the form of a pictorial pun or rebus. For example, a pub in Crowborough, East Sussex, called The Crow and Gate has an image of a crow with gates as wings.

Most British pubs still have decorated signs hanging over their doors, and these retain their original function of enabling the identification of the public house. Today's pub signs almost always bear the name of the pub, both in words and in pictorial representation.

Still not convinced that pubs can tell us something about our past? Well think again! Take for example the name 'The Royal Oak'. A survey carried out in the 1980s showed that this was the second most popular pub name in the country (the first being the 'Red Lion'). As most people know, the pub owes its name to King Charles II. After his defeat at the Battle of Worcester in 1651 he hid in an oak tree at Boscobel House near Wolverhampton. With the restoration of the monarchy, the King declared that his birthday, 29 May, would be celebrated as 'Royal Oak Day'. From that moment on pubs took on the name of the Royal Oak in what appears to be genuine thanksgiving at the restoration. The Talbot is also a popular name for a pub, indeed you will find one in the pages of this book. The pictorial representation associated with the name is a variety of hound formerly used for hunting. Its name derives from the fifteenth century Talbot family, who used the hound on their coat of arms. Another popular but unusual pub name is the Hogshead. Pubs with this name are named after the large casks of various capacities used for wines and beers which were known as a hogshead! One of our favourite names is the Bottle and Glass, a fairly obvious name for a pub you may think. This name dates from the late seventeenth century, when beer in bottles was very much a novelty. Innkeepers were very anxious to show they were up to date and to advertise this fact, and so the name became popular.

Perhaps it is not surprising that so many pubs are haunted, or at least have the reputation of being so. Ghosts, like pubs, generate strong views. You either believe in them or you don't. The great ghost hunter James Wentworth Day, writing in 1972 said, 'No house should be more haunted than an ancient inn. If one was to take a minute survey of the haunted houses of England, it is more than likely that the old inns would beat the moated granges not by a short head but by a few lengths.'

... And Spirits

Most of us have at some time been asked, or have asked the question, do you believe in ghosts? On the face of it, this is a strange question in view of the fact that ghosts, apparitions and poltergeists have been reported all over the world for thousands of years, often by people whose word we would accept without question on any other matter.

Perhaps the question is best put another way, do you accept that people have experienced encounters with what they believe to be ghosts? Even the most hardened rationalist would have difficulty in saying no! The distinction is important because it leaves open the controversial issue of whether there are ghosts out there occupying space or whether they are hallucinations.

For as long as men and women have buried their dead, they have imagined their return. But what is a ghost? How do we define what we mean by the term ghost? Historically, the word can be traced back to Indo-European ghois or gheis, which also produced the Old Norse word geisa meaning rage, and the Gothic word usgaisjan meaning terrify. The Old English form of the word was gast, which in Middle English became gost. The 'gh' spelling was probably inspired by the Flemish gheest and first appeared at the end of the fifteenth century. In the Middle Ages, the word ghost was simply a synonym for spirit or soul. It did not acquire its modern connotation of the disembodied spirit of a dead person appearing to the living until the fourteenth century. But what do we mean when we say ghost? Many great minds in psychical research have grappled with this tricky definition, but perhaps the best description is used by the parapsychologist Michael Thalbourne: 'A sensory experience in which there appears to be present a person or animal (deceased or living) who is in fact out of sensory range of the experient.'

For those who believe that ghosts are purely the spirits of the dead, the categorisation of ghosts and apparitions undertaken by G. N. M. Tyrrell in the 1940s is certainly food for thought. Tyrell was an electrical engineer who had worked with Marconi and was an influential psychical researcher. He divided reports of apparitions into four separate categories; experimental apparitions, crisis apparitions, post-mortem apparitions and finally ghosts. The first category (experimental) refers to cases where a living person attempts to project an apparition of themselves to another living person. The second category (crisis) concerns people who are undergoing a crisis of some kind, such as a life threatening illness or accident and who appear to the living at the time of the crisis. Tyrell's third category is the post-mortem apparition, and this involves the likeness of a person who is known to have been dead for at least twelve hours appearing to a living witness. The final category is the ghost. For Tyrell, there was an important difference between post-mortem apparitions and ghosts. Ghosts appear to haunt a specific location, indeed to be place centred, and to be less aware of their surroundings.

As we have seen with Tyrell's first category, sightings of ghosts are not always of the dead. In the 1880s, the Society for Psychical Research carried out a large scale study of ghosts and apparitions. Members of the public were asked, 'Have you ever, when believing yourself to be completely awake, had a vivid impression of seeing, or being touched by a living or inanimate object, or of hearing a voice, which impression, so far as you could discover, was not due to any external physical cause?' The 17,000 replies the Society received showed that about one person in ten answered yes. Of all of the results received, the majority of apparitions reported were apparitions of the living. Apparitions of the living are also known as doppelgangers, or by the more technical sounding, autophany.

Ghosts have a history that goes back at least as far as classical Greece; indeed the oldest known ghost story appears in the Sumerian Epic of Gilgamesh written around 2000 BC. Most of the dead in ancient Greece, such as those who died under natural circumstances and had the appropriate funeral ceremonies performed, passed peacefully into the realms of Hades. But some of the dead (such as those who died untimely or violent deaths) remained trapped between the two worlds.

The respected historian Keith Thomas has this to say about historical accounts of ghosts. 'In medieval England it was fully accepted that dead men might sometimes return to haunt the living.' He notes that the Catholic Church of the time rationalised this belief by regarding such apparitions as the souls of those trapped in Purgatory. On the other hand, early Protestant preachers regarded ghosts as either popish fraud or demons. To ask someone in the sixteenth century whether or not they believed in ghosts was akin to asking if they believed in transubstantiation or the papal supremacy. Such things were just taken for granted.

An interesting question seldom asked by many people interested in ghosts is why do tales of Pre-Reformation monks, sixteenth century Elizabethans and seventeenth century Civil War ghosts predominate over those from later eras? More crucially, why do people only start seeing ghosts of people from earlier periods after about 1680? Indeed, such sightings are rare until the late nineteenth century. The folklorist Jeremy Harte makes this poignant observation, that nobody saw the ghosts of Roman soldiers in Dorset until the arrival of mass education taught the public that there had been such things as Roman soldiers and then they started popping up all over the place.

The most popular explanation for a ghost is the spirit hypothesis. In its simplest form, it suggests that a ghost is the spirit or soul of a person that survives bodily death. There are a variety of explanations as to why the spirit of a person should return after death; an attachment to the location or a person they are haunting, a call for assistance (perhaps to help the spirit deal with unfinished business) or the intent on behalf of the ghost to offer comfort to a loved one.

An alternative paranormal explanation to this is the super-ESP hypothesis, which suggests that ghosts are not the spirits of the dead, but are the result of a telepathic communication from a living or dying person to the witness. Memories about the deceased person are projected by ESP (extra-sensory perception) from those who knew them to the person who is having the apparitional experience. This was a popular theory among the Victorian Cambridge academics such as Frederick Myers and Edmund Gurney who founded the Society for Psychical Research in 1882. In recent years it has become less popular.

Another theory is that ghosts are the recordings of past events, somehow recorded onto the fabric of a building or local environment. This has become known as the Stone Tape Theory after the 1970s TV drama, 'The Stone Tape' by Nigel Kneale. Like many theories for ghosts and apparitions, this theory is much older than its 1970s namesake. The theory became popular through the support of the Victorian scientist Sir Oliver Lodge, Professor of Physics and Mathematics at Liverpool University and Principal of Birmingham University. Lodge suggested that grief and suffering are recorded onto the ether at the place where these emotions occurred, and are somehow played back at a later date.

The majority of the stories presented here were obtained at first hand from pub staff and customers, many of whom had experienced the phenomena directly for themselves. As such, they form a unique anecdotal heritage record of Black Country haunted hostelries both past and present.

One of the most difficult parts of this book has been deciding what to put in and what to leave out. No book, no matter how well researched, can hope to be completely comprehensive. Inevitably there will be pubs which you know to be haunted which are not in these pages. If there are, then we would like to hear from you. There are also pubs, such as The Blue Ball, Oldbury, which had a strong reputation for being haunted. Sadly this pub has gone the way of many Black Country hostelries, and is no longer standing (a commercial business now stands on the site). As tempting as it has been, we have tried to list pubs that are still pubs or are closed but still have the possibility of re-claiming their former glory.

Ghosts are in general treated, at best, with good natured tolerance and amusement by the public. To some, there is a natural explanation when greeted with stories of haunted pubs – the witnesses concerned have had too much to drink. Edmund Gurney, one of the founders of the Society for Psychical Research in 1882 had this to say about such explanations:

> The reply of average common-sense to any account of an apparition is usually either that the witness is lying or grossly exaggerating, or that he was mad or drunk or emotionally excited at the time; or that the very most that his experience was an illusion – a misinterpretation of some insight or sound which was of an entirely objective kind. A very little careful study of the subject will, however, show that all these hypotheses must often be rejected.

And this is also our view.

As you settle yourself down to read the stories in this book, remember that ghosts are a complex phenomenon, worthy of your serious attention. If you are looking for an explanation to the stories you read in these pages, perhaps you would be wise to remember that for those that believe in ghosts no explanation is needed, and for those who don't, no explanation is possible.

Badgers Sett
A456 Kidderminster Road, Pedmore, Stourbridge, DY9 9JS

The Badgers Sett has, like most pubs, undergone several changes over the years, not least in its name which for many years was The Gypsy's Tent. It now houses a restaurant and a Travel Inn is also on site for those brave enough to stay in the area at night.

During the latter years of the Second World War, Stourbridge was gripped by a grisly mystery. One sunny April day in 1943, four schoolboys discovered the remains of a skeleton in a Wych Elm tree in nearby Hagley Wood. One of them, Bob Farmer, remembers, 'On the forehead there was a small patch of rotting flesh with lank hair attached to it and the two front teeth were crooked.' The skeleton's mouth was stuffed with taffeta and a gold wedding ring. Some crepe shoes were found nearby. Most grisly of all, one of her hands had been cut off. Terrified, the four young lads were too frightened to mention the shocking discovery to anyone. It was a few days later that their parents discovered the full story. Even with the full force of a police investigation the identity of the skeleton remained a mystery.

Examination by the pathologist, Professor James Webster, suggested that the skeleton was female, aged about thirty-five, five feet tall, with brown hair. She had given birth at least once and had died approximately two years earlier in October 1941. The coroner confirmed it was murder with asphyxiation as the probable cause of death. As for the skeleton, it went missing after Professor Webster bequeathed it to a friend at Birmingham University Medical School.

Badgers Sett.

Theories abound. Was she a war time German spy? A murdered lover? A victim of witchcraft? The witchcraft theory found favour with the influential folklorist, Professor Margaret Murray, of University College, London. Support for the spy theory came a few years later in 1953, when a local journalist was approached by a woman calling herself 'Anna'. She claimed that Bella was in fact Clarabella Dronkers, who had been killed for knowing too much about a pro-German spy ring in the Stourbridge area. She said that two German parachutists had landed and vanished in the area in early 1941. The spy ring had included a Dutchman, a foreign trapeze artist and a British officer, who had died insane in 1942. It could almost be an Alfred Hitchcock film.

In more recent years graffiti has appeared in and around Stourbridge asking the chilling question 'Who put Bella in the Wych Elm?' During the investigation, the police based their investigations from the pub, which was then called The Gypsy's Tent (a name it held until a few years ago). In 1999, an article by Richard Askwith on the Bella in the Wych Elm mystery appeared in *The Independent*. A previously unpublished story about the ghost of Bella collected by David Taylor was even mentioned. The story caught the imagination of composer Simon Holt, who was inspired to write an opera called 'Who Put Bella in the Wych Elm'. In this forty-five minute piece, reflecting on the gruesome event, he has an elderly man who witnessed the killing but did not come forward at the time, detailing the story until the ghost of Bella herself puts in an appearance.

In the 1970s, in his childhood school holidays, David Taylor, one of the authors, would often accompany his mother who worked in the pub as a waitress – the chefs and bar staff loved to tell him stories about the local ghost, who they called Bella. Live-in staff claimed that at night, lights would be turned on and off, objects moved, and doors would open and close of their own accord. All of these spooky occurrences were blamed on 'Bella'. It was not until many years later that David discovered that the local nickname given to the skeleton discovered in Hagley wood was 'Bella'. So does she still haunt the pub today? If she does, then she is in good company, as staff have also recently reported the ghost of a gentleman in a tweed jacket seen by staff and customers inside the pub.

But perhaps the real ghostly associations with the pub are on the A456 that runs past the pub. In the ten years that Parasearch have been monitoring this stretch of road, they have received all manner of ghostly reports. If all of these are to be believed, and we see no reason why not, then the short stretch of road outside the pub is haunted by a woman in white, a Civil War Cavalier, a figure in grey, a phantom hound and a mysterious black mass by the side of the road.

Beacon Hotel
Bilston Street, Sedgley, DY3 1JE

The Beacon Hotel is a very traditional Victorian Black Country pub and great pains are taken to preserve its distinctive character. To make sure that the pub remains unspoilt, Sarah Hughes, who gives her name to the present day brewery, keeps watch from her portrait in the sitting room.

The Beacon was built in 1850 along with its three storey brew house which was working continually until 1958. The pub (officially 'hotel') was bought by Sarah Hughes in 1921 after her husband's death in a mining accident. She took it over as a widow with ten children but already had experience of brewing at the 'Plume of Feathers' next to Hanson's Brewery in Dudley. Sarah held the license for thirty years and it passed on through her family where it remains to the present day. Brewing started again in 1987 using Sarah's award winning recipe for Dark Ruby Mild.

A past manager of the Beacon, Andrew, tells this story:

In the summer of 1994 when I was managing the Beacon I often used to stay overnight for security. I usually slept in the sitting room. In that room is a painting of Sarah Hughes in which the eyes seem to follow you around the room. I suppose you never sleep properly when you are on protection duty, and one night something woke me. My alarm clock showed 3.00am. Opening my eyes, I took a quick glance around the room. In the corner by the door to the passage stood a figure. After a couple of seconds I realised they had not broken into the pub or the alarms would be shrieking. I don't know how long I looked at the figure. It was a man in his 50s wearing wellington

Beacon Hotel.

boots, dark trousers and a grey or white shirt with an old fashioned Grandad style collar and a waistcoat. I have always thought that ghosts were transparent, but he looked quite solid. Suddenly grasping what I was seeing, my heart raced and I shut my eyes tight. When I looked again a few seconds later the figure had vanished. I told my father about the night visitor and described what he was wearing. He said it sounded like the father of the present owner who always liked to go about in old fashioned clothes.

Paul is another past manager of the Beacon and claims that he has seen Sarah Hughes herself. She was walking across the smoke room and through a wall where there is now a conservatory. Fifty years ago there was a door at this point.

Paul also says that if you stand in the corridor near the main servery and listen carefully, you might hear bumps and bangs from upstairs and the noise of someone standing on a loose floor board, though those rooms are used only for storage. Many regular customers claim to have heard the noises. In fact one of the authors, Andrew Homer, heard them when we were researching this book. 'At first I took no notice of the sounds, though they were quite loud. It sounded as though someone was moving heavy barrels about upstairs.' Later the same evening a casual remark to Adrian, the barman, revealed the story and confirmed that there had definitely been no living person upstairs at the time.

Bottle and Glass
Black Country Living Museum, Tipton Road, Dudley, DY1 4SQ

The Bottle and Glass was moved to the Black Country Living Museum from Brierley Hill Road, Brockmoor. It used to stand near to the Stourbridge canal at the top of the 'sixteen' locks. The exact age of the pub is not known but it is likely it was built about the same time as the canal in the late eighteenth century. The original name was the Bush, but by the 1840s it was known as the 'Bottle and Glass' and kept this name until the pub closed in 1979. Over the years the pub had only been superficially modernised so the Museum have been able to restore the pub with its original timber seating to how it would have looked in the 1870s.

The Bottle and Glass was presented to the Museum in 1979 by Ansells Brewery. It was dismantled brick by brick and re-constructed in its present location in the Museum's village. It is once again a fully functioning public house serving traditional local cask conditioned beers. A few minor changes to comply with environmental health regulations have had to be made but essentially the pub retains its old Black Country atmosphere.

Minnie Holden, who was born in 1904, visited the Bottle and Glass in 1984 and provided the following information about the haunting of the pub. As a young child, Minnie had lived at the pub with her Aunt and Uncle, a Mr and Mrs Hilton, who kept the Bottle and Glass from 1914 to 1928. After living with another Aunt in Birmingham, at the age of twenty Minnie returned to the pub again to live with her

Bottle and Glass.

Aunt Lucy. The pub must have been a colourful and at times rowdy environment for a young lady as it was frequented by miners, bargees and glass blowers.

Often canal boatmen would stay drinking all day and there were frequent drunken brawls and fights. Hardly a suitable place for a young lady! Minnie remembered that the smallest of the three bedrooms (originally a store room) was reputedly haunted by an unseen entity. No ghost was ever seen but things would frequently go missing and the room always had a strange unnerving feeling to it. On one occasion Minnie's Aunt Lucy and her daughter-in-law were sleeping in this room and awoke in the morning to find all their clothes and bedclothes piled up in the corner of the room by some unseen hands. This was all too much for the daughter-in-law who left for home without delay!

Staff at the Black Country Living Museum believe the pub to still be haunted despite being moved from its original location. Strange, inexplicable noises have been heard at times but as yet nothing has been seen.

Highgate Brewery Stores
Walsall, High Street, Walsall, WS1 1QR

The Brewery Stores is an imposing Victorian building with many of the original features still intact. It is in an area of Walsall which has a colourful history going right back to medieval times. Indeed, the market which runs along the High Street outside the pub dates back to medieval times and it is believed that the Brewery Stores was built on a burgage plot (a plot which would have been leased to a trader on the market).

When the Brewery Stores was being renovated by the Highgate Brewery an old rotten set of stocks was found in the cellar. Further research on this revealed that an area further down the High Street on the opposite side of the market was used for the punishment of minor crimes by placing people in the stocks.

Between January and March 1998 the Highgate Brewery employed various contractors to completely renovate the Brewery Stores to its present condition. Right from when the workmen first moved in there were complaints of things going missing and tools being moved. At first it was just assumed a fellow workman was playing practical jokes but all this was to change after the events of Friday 13 in February of 1998.

One of the workmen, Rob, was on his own down in what was to become the Cellar Bar tidying up his tools at the end of the day. Out of the corner of his eye he noticed something at the end of the bar nearest the main street. He looked up to see what it was and was confronted by the disembodied head of an elderly, bearded man. He had a hood pulled over his head but no other part of his body could be seen. The workman looked away for a split second to see if anyone else had come down into the cellar, but he was alone apart from the spectral figure. By now thoroughly terrified by the experience, he quickly left the building and steadfastly refused to go

Highgate Brewery Stores.

back down the cellar unless accompanied by other workmen and with all the lights on. It turned out that other workmen had experienced a funny, cold atmosphere down in the cellar and no-one liked working down there alone.

A DJ working for Vault Radio broadcasting from the Cellar Bar suddenly felt very cold one evening and went to put on his overcoat. When he came back he went to pick his headphones up and they mysteriously moved away from him as if pushed by unseen hands. While locking up late one night a member of staff went down to the cellar to turn things off. While down there the sound of a very heavy bench being moved across a wooden floor was heard though nothing could be seen and nothing had moved. More recently a member of staff who works in the Cellar Bar has seen a shadowy figure pass across the vaults end of the room on at least two occasions.

The cellar certainly isn't the only active area in the pub as an apparition described by a past resident as an 'old lady' is said to walk around the first floor and the kitchen. One of the chefs, while chopping vegetables, saw the reflection of a 'misty figure' pass straight through the wall.

The Britannia Inn
Kent Street, Upper Gornal, DY3 1UX

The Britannia Inn is better known locally as 'Sallies' after Sallie Williams who ran the pub right up until her death in 1991. In common with many public houses dating back to the early nineteenth century, the Britannia came into existence as an inn thanks to the Duke of Wellington's Beerhouse Act of 1830. This permitted householders to turn a private house into a public house on payment of two guineas. Sedgley nail maker John Jukes opened the Britannia in his small terraced house in 1832.

At one point in its history the Britannia was also home to a butcher's shop when one Henry Perry took over in 1864. He sold meat at the front of the shop and beer around the back. Sallie inherited the pub in 1942 and ran it with her husband who became the brewer. Dark, heavy, strong mild is traditionally popular in this area and it is for this that Walter 'Wally' Williams is best remembered. His Gornal Old Ale (nicknamed 'Cow and Gate') was brewed on the premises up until 1959. When Sallie passed away in 1997 she ended a family involvement with the pub going back 127 years. In all this time the Britannia has changed little and remains a hostelry steeped in local history and character.

The Britannia has played host to much ghostly activity since Sallie's death in 1991. After Landlord Stan and his wife Sigi took over the pub, their two German Shepherd dogs would often stand at the entrance to the cellar but never dare venture down. On one occasion, the dogs got Sigi out of bed and led her to the cellar entrance downstairs. Thinking someone may have got in through the dray hatch she bravely went down into the cellar to check but there was no-one there. In the lounge bar the older dog would often come in and appear to follow someone as if they were walking around the room.

Things also go missing or turn up in strange places. On one occasion Sigi left a sum of money from the sale of a piano on the lounge table. The pub was closed and locked up at the time with only the landlord and landlady on the premises. Returning five minutes later, Sigi found that the money had completely disappeared. To this day the money has never been found. On another occasion Sigi took off her wristwatch prior to taking a bath and put it beside the sink in the bathroom. When she got out of the bath the watch had gone. It materialised again some six weeks later. It was found placed on a wall unit in the front room of the pub where it would have been easily spotted by the cleaners. Stan also had his wallet removed from the bedside table one night. This turned up two days later in the pocket of a suit stored in the spare room.

Watch out for things moving by mysterious unseen hands in the bar. A hanging glass has been seen to swing violently from side to side and only stop when someone puts their hand on it. A small cannon which sits on the fireplace has also been known to suddenly fly off and land somewhere in the room.

Much activity is centred around the ladies toilets, which at one time would have been part of the old kitchen. Even with the heating turned on the toilets always seem colder than the rest of the pub and perhaps with good reason. Two apparitions have been seen here on a number of occasions. One night two girls accompanied each other to the ladies but soon came flying out of the door again.

The Britannia Inn.

On entering they had been confronted by the figure of a very old lady dressed all in black. Apparently, the two young ladies have never been seen in the pub since! On other occasions visitors to the ladies have been amazed to see a little girl dressed in Victorian style clothes, with a small black and white dog sitting on the window ledge. Ladies usually go to the toilet in pairs at the Britannia for good reason.

Bush Inn
Summit Place, Gornal Wood, DY3 2TG

The Bush Inn is a warm and friendly pub. The plates, horse brasses, harnesses and other knick knacks give the pub an 'olde worlde' ambience. It is also a pub that is back to front. The traditional pub exterior belies the fact that in the eighteenth century the front of the pub faced the other way. This becomes obvious once you venture out into the beer garden at the rear and view the impressive doorway and steps. In fact the pub started life as a stone built Georgian terrace, before Stephen Hales became the pub's first landlord in 1820.

Strange things have been happening at the Bush ever since anyone can remember. For licensee John and his partner Kim, ghostly goings on began soon after they moved into the pub in November 2000. John was standing behind the bar when he

Bush Inn.

felt something heavy press against the back of his legs. Thinking it was their Red Setter he was shocked to discover that nothing was there when he turned around. Not wishing to scare his partner or staff, John decided to keep the experience to himself. A few months later one of the barmaids, Linda, had the same experience but this time in the corridor leading from the bar to the toilets. It wasn't long before other members of staff were reporting similar experiences.

Anita was cleaning the pub one morning when she felt an invisible spectral dog brush past her legs. Pub regular Keith thinks he may have actually seen the spectral hound when he saw a black Labrador disappear up the corridor leading to the toilets.

Stories that the pub is haunted began to circulate among the locals when a loud bang was heard by regulars in the bar in December 2002. The noise was so loud they thought it was a repetition of the Gornal earthquake and rushed outside. Neighbours in houses opposite also heard the bang and came out to see what was happening. Strangely, there appeared to be nothing at all amiss.

If the regulars had any doubts that the pub was haunted these came to an end in July 2003 when an ornamental plate jumped off the wall in front of a pub full of regulars and landed a few feet away, unbroken!

These strange goings on have not been confined to opening hours. One night in bed, John's partner Kim awoke and was horrified to see a lady in Victorian dress glide across the bedroom. Kim later said, 'I was thinking I must be dreaming but the bedroom looked exactly the same as it does in reality.' Kim was puzzled to notice that the phantom lady appeared rather short, but this puzzle was soon solved. The level of their bedroom floor, which is on the ground floor, had been altered and is now higher than it was in Victorian times. Former landlady, Sonya, has also admitted that her mother has seen the ghost of a Victorian lady while she stayed at the pub.

Stan and Pat were licensees of the pub for over ten years. Not surprisingly they have some strange stories to tell. During their time at the pub they regularly heard knocks and banging as well as footsteps coming from the attic. The sound of barrels being moved in the cellar was also a regular occurrence. But most interestingly of all, their daughter, Lynn, reportedly saw the ghost of a little old lady in her own bedroom.

Suggestions that the pub is haunted, not just by a phantom dog but also a female spirit, came one night after closing time when Stan and his brothers were downstairs in the bar having a drink. They were surprised to hear the sound of a female voice coming from the front room. Thinking that a regular had been locked in, Stan went to investigate. Although he searched high and low he found no one there, although he did notice it was extremely cold and the family dog refused to enter the room. Many years ago this room had been the 'Ladies Room', when it was considered that the bar was not a nice place for genteel ladies to frequent.

Another brush with the female phantom came when Stan was playing his electronic organ. So he could practice, Stan would record himself playing and then play the tape back so he could listen and improve on his technique. While he was playing back the tape one day he distinctly heard the voice of a woman say 'Divine'. Apart from Stan the room was empty at the time (of other living souls that is).

So, if you happen to pop into the Bush for a drink, don't be too surprised if you feel a spectral dog brush past you.

Feline and Firkin
Princess Street, Wolverhampton, WV1 1HW

The Feline and Firkin has gone through a number of changes over the years and used to be called The Greyhound. For a town centre pub it has an unusual claim to fame. It is said to be the only one in Wolverhampton city centre to boast a proper beer garden.

Watch out in this pub for the apparition seen behind the bar is none other than a member of Her Majesty's constabulary in full uniform! Perhaps there to apprehend the other apparition seen at the pub, one Jack The Hat, a villainous name if ever there was one. A visitor here could well be treated to the spectacle of spectral cops and robbers!

The Fountain Inn
Owen Street, Tipton, DY4 8HE

A ghostly sighting in the attic of this pub many years ago has led to speculation that the spirit of William Perry, 'The Tipton Slasher' may haunt his old training ground.

The Fountain Inn.

Statue of William Perry, 'The Tipton Slasher'.

A quite remarkable sighting occurred here some years ago, when the landlord, his wife and others saw something strange in the attic. 'I have vivid memories of a man seated in a chair,' begins one witness, 'wearing just boxing shorts, his hair jet black in colour with a middle parting and of course, a handlebar moustache.' The ghostly figure disappeared as mysteriously as it had appeared, leaving everyone mystified.

The pub had been the training headquarters for William Perry, known to everyone as 'The Tipton Slasher'. Could it be that he still haunts the pub? Unfortunately the description given does not seem to match that of Perry himself, but one thing is certain, something strange was seen in that attic many years ago.

Giffard Arms
Victoria Street, Wolverhampton, WV1 3NX

The Giffard Arms is situated in the busy centre of Wolverhampton surrounded by shops. The building was originally commissioned in 1922 and built in the Tudor style. Before that a coach house stood on the same site.

Giffard Arms.

There are a number of ghosts said to haunt The Giffard including that of a previous landlord. One of the most interesting is reputed to be Anne Horton, a local 'lady of the night', who used to give her favours away. Her ghostly form has been known to follow young men home from the pub – you have been warned!

The Locomotive Inn
Vicar Street, Dudley

Stories that the Locomotive was haunted began in the early 1980s when a barmaid, who was living there at the time, fell victim to the resident poltergeist one night: 'I was awoken by something or somebody resting on the bed,' the barmaid said. 'I felt the bedclothes being pulled away from me, I pulled them back and turned my face to the wall. 'It' seemed to come around the other side, towards where my face was. 'It' seemed to want to pull the bed clothes off my face. This only lasted a couple of seconds and I just lay there, still. I couldn't move until the light shone in the room as daylight broke.'

Besides this, other classic poltergeist activity has taken place, such as furniture and other objects being moved without anyone touching them; doors opening and closing of their own accord; and as the then Landlady Mrs Pauline Leadbetter reported, 'My husband's yard-glass has shattered as it hung on the wall; I've gone to put a roast in the oven and the door slammed on me and burned me; and my jewellery has come off my neck without being broken.'

The ghost is said to be that of a previous owner, one who may not be entirely happy when changes are made, as Pauline Leadbetter remarks, 'Strange things always happen when we've been decorating, or making any changes to the pub, like strange smells. I've gone to change a barrel down the cellar and I've felt as though someone has got a grip on me although there's nobody there.'

Ye Olde Boat Inn
Cradley Road, Netherton

A report from 1975 suggests that this old Netherton ale-house may have a haunted reputation tinged with dark and foul deeds.

Mr Leshon grew up in the pub that his parents owned when he was a child. The locals talked of a grisly murder that took place in the pub cellars many years before. It was said that two brothers were in the cellars when an argument began over money, and one had killed the other with an axe and buried the body under the cellar floor. The body had not been discovered until many years later, and the murderer was brought to justice for his crime and was hanged.

Not surprisingly after that, the pub had a reputation of being haunted. Mr Leshon remembers mysterious things going on in the pub when he was a child, 'I can still remember the strange things which occurred. Shadows on the wall and voices in the cellar. I can remember lying awake in bed at night, and hearing the strange noises and the heavy tread of footsteps descending the cellar stairs.' Other members of the Leshon family also had strange experiences in the pub. Mr Leshon remembers, 'My mother also heard and saw things in the place. She told us that when she was alone in the living room the bolts on the door were withdrawn by an unseen hand, the door opened of its own accord and then shut again!'

Old Bulls Head Inn
Redhall Road, Lower Gornal, DY3 2NU

The Old Bulls Head is a traditional Black Country pub, full of local charm and a friendly welcome. In common with other pubs in the area, the Old Bulls Head started life in the nineteenth century as a butcher's, which also brewed and sold beer.

Old Bulls Head Inn.

There have been a variety of paranormal experiences reported in the pub over the years. A previous landlord reported that the pub juke box used to play on its own even when it was not plugged in! Former landladies Jenny Newton and Linda Chapman also reported a variety of strange experiences.

One of the first incidents to happen to them bore all the hallmarks of a poltergeist, or noisy or mischievous spirit. In a closed and locked bar the two owners found a book on one of the bar tables, which appeared to have been placed open. Linda remembers that the book had been on the bookshelf, and that if it had fallen it would have landed on the floor, not open on the table. A few days later Linda was in the bar cleaning. She noticed a beer mat on the floor, so picked it up and put it on the table. She carried on dusting, but on turning round she found the beer mat was on the floor again. This happened a further four times! Another classic poltergeist trait is that keys and other objects disappear and reappear in unusual places.

Other experiences suggest that there may be more than a poltergeist at play in the pub. Sudden temperature drops have been experienced by staff and customers in the bar, apparently for no reason at all. The distant tones of strange music have been heard in the early hours of the morning from an untraceable source, a phenomena which was also witnessed by a previous tenant of the pub.

While you are sitting down enjoying a pint don't be too scared if you see a shadowy figure pass by. On several occasions customers in the bar have seen an unknown figure going upstairs. When staff have checked there has been no one there! Could this be connected to the figure Linda has seen walking across the upstairs landing? On another occasion, late one night after locking the lounge, Linda and a customer both saw through the dividing window a figure dressed in green walking around in the lounge. Yet again, upon investigation there was nobody there.

There are reputed to be three ghosts at the Old Bulls Head. They are a man in the cellar, a lady in red outside the stable area at the back of the pub and a lady in grey. Who could these ghosts be? It is said that there had been an old coaching house at the rear of the pub many years ago and that one of the maids had a steamy affair with the stable lad. It is unclear if he was already married or was engaged to someone else, but the story goes he cruelly rejected her and she committed suicide by hanging herself in the old brewery which is still connected to the pub.

The Old Bulls Head is certainly a strange building, and is it any wonder, as it is situated in a very haunted area of the Black Country. Nearby are a variety of haunted sites, including a school, shops, houses, roads and even a church. In 1881, the Reverend Rooker of nearby St James Church was assaulted by a supernatural attacker as he walked home through the churchyard. The event caused quite a panic in the neighbourhood and was even reported in the *Daily Telegraph*. Both police and locals hid out in the churchyard in an attempt to either catch the attacker or glimpse the ghost. Although they didn't catch anyone they did hear ghostly voices and caught glimpses of shadowy figures flitting between the grave stones. You may want to think twice before taking a short cut home after your visit to this pub!

The Old Bush
Skidmore Road, Coseley, WV14 8SE

Whatever, or whoever, haunts The Old Bush seems to have a fondness for a particular glass. One glass in particular falls on the floor from the shelf but never breaks. The ghost, said to be an unknown male, moves and throws the glass, but for some strange reason it never breaks. Psychic investigator David Dornan said: 'If necessary we will spend a night in any particular room supposedly haunted with recording equipment and infra-red photographic gear.'

The Old Mill
Windmill Street, Ruiton, Gornal, DY3 2DQ

The Old Mill as the name suggests has associations with one of two windmills which once graced the Gornal skyline. The brick structure of Ruiton windmill can still be seen in nearby Vale Street but no trace remains of the windmill which gave this pub its name.

In common with many pubs recorded here, The Old Mill lays claim to phantom noises and things being moved around when there is no-one in the pub. In 1998 local paranormal research group, Parasearch, was called in to investigate just such

The Old Mill.

goings on at the Mill. On this occasion, during the night odd bumps and bangs were indeed heard by members of the group. At the time no obvious explanations were apparent until one memorable incident in the early hours of the morning.

Author, Andrew Homer, happened to be sitting closest to the cellar door in the lounge. No-one was down there at the time but all of a sudden loud banging noises began emanating from the bottom of the cellar. Some readers may think running in the opposite direction a sensible move but as it was I reached the cellar door first and literally flew down the narrow steps to catch whoever, or whatever, it was. On reaching the floor of the cellar the culprit was right there in front of me. An ice machine was busy machine gunning its contents into a large metal tray!

Old Still Inn
King Street, Wolverhampton, WV1 1ST

The Old Still Inn was built in the early 1750s as a private residence. By 1833, the building belonged to Richard Hershaw and was being used as a tavern called the Old Saracen's Head. It is rumoured that Prince Albert may have visited the pub though this may have originated from Queen Victoria's visit in 1866 to unveil a statue to the recently deceased Prince Consort.

By 1896, the name had changed to the The Old Still Inn. At this time it was owned by Jacob James Tate, a Scottish wine and spirits merchant, who lived there with his wife Maria and daughter Maggie. In later years, Maggie became known as the world famous Soprano, Dame Maggie Teyte. In more recent years the pub has maintained links with show business by entertaining stars from The Grand. Among others, Les Dawson was said to be a regular visitor to the pub when he was performing at the nearby theatre.

There have been two tragic deaths by hanging in the pub. Sometime in the 1900s the Licensee hung himself. His presence is still felt in the bar, with cold spots and optics being pulled from the wall. Ashtrays and other objects also get moved around as has been witnessed by one of the licensees, John. At times the pub has a strange and very atmospheric Victorian feel to it, despite modern refurbishment. Perhaps there is an element of time-slip at work here as the pub is reputed to be the oldest surviving hostelry in Wolverhampton town centre.

The second hanging is said to be that of a young child though no further details of the circumstances are known. Suffice to say that at times the child is to be heard sobbing from one of the upper floors of the building. Could the unquiet spirits of these two poor souls still be trapped in the pub with the only way of alerting customers to their presence being by violent psychic disturbance?

If you visit this pub keep a lookout also for Martha sitting in the left hand corner of the bar. She is often mistaken for an old customer, and old she certainly is as she died in the pub sometime in the nineteenth century.

Old Still Inn.

Pie Factory
Hurst Lane, Tipton, West Midlands, DY4 9AB

The Pie Factory is a good old fashioned Black Country pub. It has a solid and reliable look about it, much like the regulars. The pub is renowned for its famous cow pies which have the reputation of being only for the truly hungry, and should not be tackled by the faint hearted!

The cellars are without doubt the most haunted part of the pub, with three ghosts associated with them. The first is Nobby, a possible former landlord who hung

The Pie Factory.

himself in the cellar. Dressed in a long black cloak, he occasionally wanders from the cellar and has the unnerving habit of pulling the shirts of gentlemen in the toilets.

The second ghost in the cellar is a little girl; she can, on occasions, be heard singing. Although her spirit has never been seen beyond the cellar, she can often be heard running up the steps and laughing.

The third ghost is more obscure and is generally described as a cavalier although he may be simply be a misidentification of Nobby doing his ghostly rounds.

The Plough Inn
School Road, Trysull, WV5 7HR

The Plough Inn is a lovely sixteenth century inn situated in the ancient and picturesque village of Trysull. It comes as no surprise to learn that the pub and the area surrounding it have ghostly tales to tell.

In 2005, local paranormal research group, Parasearch, were invited to conduct an investigation at the pub. While at the building the researchers were taken to a tiny room upstairs known as the Devil's room. On entering through a latched door they were amazed to be shown examples of Tudor wall paintings. While quite common before the Reformation, surviving examples are now quite rare especially in private homes as this pub once was.

The Plough Inn.

Even more intriguing is the subject matter depicted. Along with pictures of birds and a horse being led there is the unmistakable image of a devil replete with horns, wings and a trident. He is leading another figure on a rope, possibly an animal or a child, while a smaller impish figure dances nearby. The Devil's room is aptly named!

While Parasearch didn't record any paranormal activity during their brief stay nevertheless figures have regularly been seen in and around the pub. A previous landlady saw the figure of a cowled monk dressed in a brown habit tied with a cord. This figure was described as appearing both real and solid. Indeed, the notion that ghosts are somewhat ethereal may be something of a misnomer. In many reported sightings it is not until the figure does something unusual such as disappear or pass through a solid wall that the witness realises he or she has seen a ghost.

A rapidly moving figure has also been seen in the pub together with an apparition described as a tall lady who tried to drag an unsuspecting landlord into the kitchen! More recently, staff report that they have seen a man standing at the end of the bar who inexplicably disappears. Each time this happens there is nowhere the man could have gone without staff being aware of him leaving. Who he is or why he frequents that end of the bar is something of a mystery.

Just a few yards from the pub lies the ancient village green. It is here that a previous barmaid, Caroline, from the Red Lion in Wombourne (also featured in this book) regularly used to witness an eerie sight on her return journey home after closing time. She described regularly seeing a group of children, dressed in old fashioned clothes, dancing in a circle around a tree on the green. Driving home alone late at night it comes as no surprise that she never dared to stop and investigate further.

Prince Albert Hotel
Railway Street, Wolverhampton, WV1 1LG

The Prince Albert is a large, impressive looking public house situated within easy reach of the railway station and Wolverhampton's Grand Theatre.

The haunting of The Prince Albert Hotel centres around Room 13. In the 1920s, a Miss Williams was the Landlady of the hotel. She is reputed to have worn trousers, smoked a pipe and rode a motorbike. She had a lover by the name of Anna who was in the Royal Navy. Miss Williams and Anna used to meet up in Room 13. In order to maintain discretion Miss Williams used to put a candle in the window to signal to her lover that it was safe for them to be together. Tragically, at the onset of the Second World War, Anna was killed.

Prince Albert Hotel.

Room 13 is no longer used for guests as too many people suffered disturbed nights. Frequent reports of a presence silently standing at the bottom of the bed and the flickering light of a candle in the window suggest that Miss Williams still waits for her long lost love to return.

Queen Mary Ballroom
Dudley Castle, Castle Hill, Dudley

The Queen Mary Ballroom is situated in the heart of Dudley Castle and Zoological Gardens. It qualifies for inclusion as a haunted hostelry by virtue of the fact it has been serving beer and spirits to Dudley Zoo and Castle visitors for decades.

The Dudley Castle site plays host to a plethora of ghosts from different time periods and the Queen Mary Ballroom itself has a reputation for being haunted. On occasions when the ballroom has been closed to visitors the sound of a piano being played has been clearly heard coming from within the locked building. No-one knows who the phantom pianist might be or who they might be playing for.

The ballroom is situated near to the ruined Sharingdon range which was ravaged by fire in 1750. The castle keep, at the other end of the courtyard, is where the famous Grey Lady of Dudley Castle, one Dorothy Beaumont, has been regularly sighted over the years. Dorothy was the wife of John Beaumont, the Deputy Commander of Dudley Castle, during the Parliamentarian siege of 1646. The story goes that she gave birth to a daughter, Frances, in 1645. When the child died the same year Dorothy was never to get over the loss. Frances was buried at St Edmunds known locally as 'bottom' church. Prior to the siege of 1646 Colonel Leveson, commander of the Royalist forces, had the church destroyed so it could not be used by the attacking Parliamentarian forces. When Dorothy herself died during the siege the opposing forces were gracious enough to allow her body to be buried at St Thomas's, known locally as 'top' church. Her body could not be accompanied by her grieving husband however, and she could not be buried alongside her beloved baby daughter.

It is said that Dorothy's restless spirit still roams Dudley Castle searching for her husband and daughter. The sad and lonely figure of a grey lady has often been seen in a number of locations but mainly in and around the base of the ancient keep. In recent times and on a number of occasions, patrons of the castle ghost walks have asked after the tour why there were two actresses playing the part of the Grey Lady on that part of the walk. Needless to say there is only ever one Dorothy Beaumont employed in that particular role!

Anniversary ghosts are said to only appear once a year on the same date. Dudley Castle Keep has an anniversary ghost who is said to appear on the night of Halloween itself. The story is that long ago an old lady chose to end her life by hanging or throwing herself from the top of the keep only to repeat the grisly spectacle each Halloween since. Whether she appears or not is open to speculation of course, but two police officers were left shaken and confused after being called out to investigate

Queen Mary Ballroom.

an intruder up on the keep. One officer stayed down below in case anyone tried to escape while the other climbed the narrow winding steps up to the top to take a look. As he walked from one end of the keep to the other the officer on the ground clearly saw a figure closely following his colleague as he walked along. Fully expecting to be greeted by his colleague accompanied by the intruder he was amazed to discover that that the policeman up on the keep had seen nobody else and had certainly not been closely followed as clearly observed from below. A group staging a charity Halloween ghost hunt had a very similar experience when the whole group observed a mysterious figure walking up and down the battlements.

One of the more unusual sightings occurs in the undercroft beneath the old chapel. This houses two stone coffins, one of which is said to have held the body of the notorious John De Somery. On one particular occasion a cleaner working in the undercroft saw a pair of old fashioned boots standing by the coffin. After a few seconds the ghostly boots slowly disappeared. Another cleaner, working in what used to be the tropical house, saw the figure of a little girl in old fashioned brown clothes standing outside looking in. The cleaner glanced away for a moment but in that time the figure had simply vanished. Black robed monks are also seen around the area outside the undercroft which once held an aquarium. Similar monks have also been seen in the area immediately outside the Queen Mary Ballroom.

The shop situated within the Sharingdon range also has its fair share of ghostly happenings. Things get moved or thrown around and on occasions a female figure, possibly Dorothy Beaumont herself, has been seen. The sound of horses is also sometimes heard even though there are never any horses nearby. Interestingly, an archaeological dig in the area some years ago revealed the bones of horses buried near to the shop.

Paranormal research group, Parasearch, has conducted a number of scientific investigations at the castle and were originally called in to investigate strange goings on in the quaintly named 'round house'. This is situated near the front entrance and at the time was used as temporary accommodation for 'Bonkers', a clown hired to entertain the children over the summer period. His sleep was regularly disturbed by loud knocking on the door and misty figures appearing on the stairs and in his bedroom. During the Parasearch investigation author Andrew Homer together with David Taylor's wife Carolyn and two other researchers were in the 'round house' when a very loud metallic sounding crash occurred from downstairs. Thinking major damage had occurred to something lights were turned on only to discover that nothing had moved or fallen in the tiny building.

The Queen's Head
Wordsley, High Street, Wordsley, DY8 5QS

The Queen's Head is a small, friendly pub which in recent years has undergone a major refurbishment.

The Queen's Head.

This pub is haunted by one of the more unusual ghosts we came across while researching for this book. This particular apparition has only been seen once upstairs by a previous landlord, however there are reports of people feeling a figure brush past them even though nothing is seen. Pennies placed on the bar have been known to be flicked off by unseen fingers and on one occasion a heavy cast iron pot shot off the range and crashed to the floor. The unusual thing about this ghost is that he or she likes to listen to the radio! If a radio is left playing in the cellar the ghost keeps quiet and there are no disturbances. This is no highbrow apparition though as the favourite stations are any playing pop music.

Seamus O'Donnells
Princess Street, Wolverhampton, WV1 1HQ

Seamus O'Donnells is a former traditional Irish pub situated in the centre of Wolverhampton. In common with many town centre pubs of its type it has had a number of different incarnations over the years.

The building is haunted by two unrelated ghosts. The first goes by the unlikely name of Scratching Fanny. Her real name was Frances Johnson. She had a relationship with a married man who used to keep the pub. Eventually, the married man grew tired of the hapless Frances and he had her banned from the premises. The story goes that she used to scratch at the door hoping to be let back in, but to no avail. Hence her unfortunate nickname of Scratching Fanny. If you are able to visit this pub sit near the door and listen carefully for you may just hear her ghost still trying to get back in.

The second apparition here is what is known as an anniversary ghost. That is, the haunting takes place at the same time each year. Unlike Scratching Fanny this ghost, known as George, seems to be quite a jovial character. He appears around the 15 or 16 February each year and haunts the area which is now the gent's toilets. He taps gentlemen on the shoulder while singing and joking!

Somerset House
Enville Street, Stourbridge, DY8 3TQ

Somerset House is a sturdy looking building, not far from Stourbridge's busy ring road. This traditional looking appearance belies the unusual past of this pub. In the late 1940s coffins were built on the premises for bodies that were temporarily kept in the cellar.

The pub hit the national headlines in 1998, when an unusual phenomena came to the attention of the local press. Details are obscure as to who exactly made the discovery, but someone found that pints of beer would stick to the wall! Reports soon began to circulate that the pub was haunted, but by who or what was never made clear. The landlord of the pub claimed that in the past the pub had been

Somerset House.

used to make and house coffins. Suspicions that the whole thing was a publicity stunt were dismissed by a brewery spokesman, 'Honestly, there is no trick.' The then landlord John Selwyn confirmed the phenomena, 'The glass can hang there all night.' But be warned, 'A lot of them end up smashing the pint on the floor, but that's ok because they buy more beer.'

David Taylor, one of the authors, visited the pub with members of Parasearch to carry out an investigation. They agreed with the conclusion reached by researchers from Wolverhampton University Psychology Department who concluded that the phenomena was caused by an unusual chemical reaction of the ink in the wallpaper. This very sensible and logical explanation could have meant that the story faded into obscurity, had it not been for the ghostly reports that were already associated with the pub.

The Ashwood
Sandringham Place, Wordsley, DY8 5HB

The Ashwood is a modern pub in the middle of a popular housing estate. A favourite with locals, the pub offers a Function Room which is always popular for weddings, christenings and birthdays.

The Ashwood.

Janice worked as a cleaner at The Ashwood for several years. As the only cleaner, being downstairs on her own in the empty pub was at times more than a little unnerving. On several occasions while busying herself with cleaning, Janice heard operatic singing over the sound of her own radio. Sometimes, this ethereal singing was accompanied by talking, although Janice was unable to quite work out what the voices were saying. Not surprisingly, Janice found that these experiences left her feeling scared and wary of being in the pub on her own.

Early one morning while going about her usual business, Janice was startled by the sight of a strange human like figure by one of the doors to the pub. Unable to contain her terror, Janice ran from the pub, too scared to go back in and finish tidying up. Sometime later when she had regained her courage Janice returned to the pub to tell the landlord what had happened. Although he had never experienced anything strange at The Ashwood himself, he listened patiently, until Janice mentioned the figure. Unable to contain himself, he burst out laughing and explained that the figure she had seen was not a ghost but a Guy Fawkes for Bonfire Night!

But of course this cannot explain the ghostly voices and singing she heard regularly in the pub. And you can't help but think a clue may lie in the name of one of the shops opposite – an off-licence called 'Spirits of Wordsley'.

The Barley Mow
City Road, Tividale, Oldbury, B69 1QS

The Barley Mow is perched high up overlooking Dudley and the Black Country. While the pub itself had shut down at the time of writing the building remains, now boarded up.

When the pub was a popular local hostelry, regulars used to recognise the smell of burnt toast and beer going inexplicably flat as a sure sign of ghostly activity.

Previous licensees Diane and Steve were plagued by a series of paranormal phenomena since they took over the running of the pub. The couple had gas cylinders in the cellar turned off, alarms triggered with no apparent cause and glasses thrown from shelves. Diane explains, 'Just after we moved in our dogs started to go mad for no reason – as if they were terrified. The beer started going flat so we checked the gas cylinders in the cellar and they had been turned off. Nobody had been down there.'

Former bar staff have also claimed to have caught glimpses of ghostly figures. A clairvoyant visiting the pub may have shed some light on these eerie events. She claimed that the supernatural occurrences were due to the restless spirit of one Sam Cole, who used to regularly leave his horse and cart outside the pub while he

The Barley Mow.

partook of the ale. A few days after the clairvoyant's visit, Diane asked an old pub regular about Sam Cole. He looked a bit shocked, explaining that Sam Cole was in fact Sam the Coalman. He used to be a regular at the pub, often leaving his horse and cart outside.

Psychics who have also visited the pub have sensed the presence of a young girl named Melissa, who is thought to have died when the building was part of a farm.

Paranormal Investigators from Midlands based Parasearch spent a night in the Barley Mow a few years ago. After setting up their recording equipment the team settled themselves down for the night. All was quiet until investigator Gareth Goodwin caught sight of a shadowy figure out of the corner of his eye. No one else had been in that part of the room. Unfortunately, neither was any equipment which may have recorded the phenomena.

While the group were packing up in the early hours of the morning, investigator George Gregg clearly heard the sound of a horse outside the pub. Not knowing the story of the phantom coalman George dismissed the event. Perhaps Sam Cole did indeed pay a final visit to the Barley Mow that night.

Britannia Inn
Dial Lane, West Bromwich, B70 0EF

In 1982, Teacher's, the famous whisky producer, put up £1,000 in a competition to find the region's most haunted pub.

The Britannia Inn certainly thought it was in with a chance according to the *Birmingham Evening Mail*. According to 21-year-old barmaid Olga Bailey, their resident ghost is nicknamed Ebenezer after a nearby street. According to Olga he delights in knocking glasses off shelves, turning on cookers, switching lights on and off and leaving a feeling of intense cold wherever he goes. One local, Keith Brazier, recounts an unnerving experience he had in the pub: 'I was in the toilet when it suddenly went freezing cold. I turned round and there was a tall man wearing a trilby hat and a long coat with tails. Then he just disappeared in front of my eyes.'

The Courthouse
New Street, Dudley , DY1 1LP

The Courthouse is situated right opposite the police station in the centre of Dudley and is a typical town centre hostelry.

That this pub is haunted will probably come as no surprise to anyone who knows anything about this area of Dudley. The Courthouse boasts a variety of paranormal phenomena ranging from anomalous noises to actual figures seen. Inexplicable noises are often heard coming from the cellar area, when no-one is down there.

The Courthouse.

Even more remarkably beer glasses have been known to be lifted off from the bar by some unseen hand and hover for a moment in mid-air before smashing to the floor. On one occasion, according to regular customer Ian, a figure was seen to walk across the pub as if to play pool, but there was no-one in the pool room. Sometimes the names of staff, such as employee Gail, are shouted down from upstairs even though there is nobody up there.

The Crabmill
Hagley Road, Oldswinford, DY8 2JP

The Crabmill, formerly known as The Oldswinford, is a large comfortable pub on the outskirts of Stourbridge. It hasn't always been a pub, however, as prior to the 1970s the 300 year old building had been used as a doctor's surgery. Indeed, this aspect of the building's history may shed some light on the spectral gentleman who regularly puts in an appearance here. The figure has been described as being an old gentleman, clad in a black suit and top hat. He has been seen regularly in the pub by a succession of managers and customers over the years. The general consensus of opinion seems to be that this old gentleman is still keeping a watching eye over what was possibly his former home.

The Crabmill.

More troublesome spirits also make their presence felt, or heard, in the pub and the cellars from time to time. Plates have been known to fly around in the kitchen and temporary managers particularly can often look forward to disturbed nights due to unaccountable noises coming from within supposedly empty rooms.

Local legend has it that a doctor who once owned the building committed suicide. Could this then be the old gentleman who still wanders around the pub, unable to leave the scene of his own tragic demise?

The Crooked House
Coppice Mill, Himley, DY3 4DA

The Crooked House is aptly named as nineteenth century mining subsidence has created an almost surreal atmosphere within the older parts of the pub. Originally built as a farmhouse in 1765 the property was once part of the estate of Sir Stephen Glynne whose sister, Catherine, was the wife of Prime Minister William Gladstone. The pub was once known as the Glynne Arms after this historical connection but has also been known as the Siden House. In Black Country dialect 'siden' means crooked. Despite lying next to the Earl of Dudley's estate it was Glynne himself who was responsible for the subsidence in the pursuit of revenue from the underlying coal seam.

The Crooked House is situated at the end of a long lane off the Himley Road. First time visitors often think they have taken a wrong turning as the narrow lane leads deep into Himley Wood. As soon as the Crooked House comes into view the effects of mining subsidence on this strange pub can be clearly seen. In the front room bar, marbles can be seen to apparently roll uphill on the window ledges and it is easy to lose one's balance even before any ale is sampled! It is claimed the clock is the only truly upright thing in the old part of the pub or is this just another optical illusion?

It comes as no surprise that the Crooked House is also home to at least two different apparitions. Customers often report that they 'feel something' in the older part of the pub. On occasions staff and customers have witnessed the apparition of an old man, described as being quite short and in his sixties or seventies, who enters the bar silently. At first nothing seems untoward until he is seen to simply disappear into thin air. It is thought by staff that he may be a former landlord returning to check that all is well with the pub.

A young girl in a parlour maid's outfit and cap has also been seen standing in or near the old fireplace. A visiting psychic was able to put a name to this young lady and she is known locally as Polly. Whether Polly is associated with the original farmhouse or the later public house is not known. Children have also been seen playing in the fields behind the pub – nothing unusual in that, except that these

The Crooked House.

particular children are usually seen dancing in a circle and wearing clothes that are not of this era.

The Crown
High Street, Sedgley, DY3 1RJ

The Crown is a relatively new pub being only some thirty years old. However, it replaced a much older Crown public house which existed on the same site. The present Crown is a modern, comfortable hostelry situated on the Wolverhampton side of Sedgley High Street.

The haunting of The Crown centres around one Bob Foster, a past landlord. Bob was eighteen stone and apparently died from a massive heart attack while down the cellar. A previous landlord found himself locked in his own bedroom by some unseen hand and something strange spooks dogs in the pub from time to time. On one occasion the pub dog jumped at something behind the Landlord with his hairs on end clearly scared but on turning round there was nothing to be seen.

This particular apparition also makes an appearance now and again. He has been seen in one of the toilets by a cleaner but the activity seems to centre around the cellar. Barrels can sometimes be heard being moved around although no-one

The Crown.

is down there. Two draymen had the shock of their lives when they realized that the man they had assumed to be the landlord who had stood down the cellar and shouted orders at them was none other than the long deceased Bob Foster.

The Dudley Arms
Wolverhampton Road, Himley, DY3 4LB

The Dudley Arms is a comfortable, traditional style pub, with a large car park and its own restaurant. Reports of lights being mysteriously turned on and off by unseen hands would be sufficient for the Dudley Arms to be included in this collection, but this particular hostelry is situated in an area literally steeped in history and legend. The pub was on occasion visited by Edward, Prince of Wales prior to the traumas of Kingship and Abdication that he underwent after being crowned King Edward VIII. On one particular visit to the Earl of Dudley at Himley Hall, he paid a visit to the pub with the Earl and brought everyone a drink!

But a more notorious visitor also paid a visit to the pub in the 1940s. The notorious double murderer Neville Heath stopped off at the pub in his sports car. After a drink with the locals he sped off up the Himley Road. It was weeks later that the shocked regulars saw his face splashed all over the Sunday newspapers in connection with his grizzly crimes.

Locals and regulars say that the pub is haunted by a previous landlord who is unable to let go of the fond memories he had in the pub. Whoever he may be, he is blamed for lights being turned on and off both upstairs and down.

Just down the road beyond the railway bridge lies Holbeche House which comes as quite a surprise to the unsuspecting visitor. Almost completely hidden from view, the large brick built house nestles in a woody hollow literally yards from the busy A449 Wolverhampton road. Nowadays, Holbeche is used as a nursing home, but this particular residence has not always been as quiet and peaceful as it is today. Looking back into the history of the area reveals a local ghost story plus gunpowder, treason and plot.

After Guy Fawkes was caught trying to blow up the Houses of Parliament in 1605, some of the plotters escaped and sought refuge with the Lyttleton family at Hagley Hall, some 10 miles from Holbeche. The Lyttletons were staunch Catholics and very much involved with the plot against James I, the Protestant King. The Sheriff of Worcester and his mounted militia pursued the plotters as far as Hagley and forced them on to Holbeche House, also owned by the Lyttleton family. Holbeche was chosen as a safe house for the outlaws and their servants because of its secluded location in dense woodland.

Unfortunately, while fording the river Stour at Stourbridge, a cart overturned soaking the plotter's remaining supply of gunpowder. The story goes that the sodden gunpowder was placed by a damped down open fire to dry out. Not an uncommon practice in those days. However, a careless servant thinking the house rather cold raked the fire with disastrous consequences. The resulting explosion blew off the

The Dudley Arms.

roof and severely damaged the house. The Sheriff of Worcester and his men heard the tremendous bang and mounted an immediate attack on Holbeche. Most of the remaining plotters were either killed or captured in the violent assault.

The ghost story centres on one Gideon Grove, a servant who played no part in the gunpowder plot itself. However, to the Sheriff's men he was guilty by association and hunted down in the woods to the south of Wombourne village. He was apparently trying to escape the fray by making his way back home to the village of Trysull, past where the Dudley Arms stands today. The unfortunate Gideon was pursued by the horsemen who eventually trapped their quarry in a marshy pool using pikes and spears to hold his head under the muddy water. Thus Gideon Grove met his untimely end.

On November 5, we still burn effigies of Guy Fawkes and let off fireworks to the memory of the ill-fated gunpowder plot. For many years around this time of year the ghosts of Gideon Grove and the pursuing horsemen have been heard by numerous witnesses along what is now the Bridgnorth Road (where it passes through the outskirts of Wombourne). The clamouring sounds of men and horses in full flight are heard though these particular phantoms are apparently never seen.

However, on her way home to Sedgley early one dark November evening, secretary Diane Johnson had an experience she will never forget. Having just turned right onto Himley Road she was startled by a figure which ran in front of the car and disappeared off to the left towards Himley Hall. It all happened too quickly for Diane to discern any details of the figure except that she was certain he was wearing long cavalier style boots. Even more intriguing, the figure ran across the road from the direction of Holbeche House, as if he was fleeing from some unseen menace. Where he passed in front of the car is a very long, tall fence which borders Himley Hall. There is no gap in this fence where the figure could have passed through had he been a real live person. Diane is not the only motorist to have seen spectral figures from the past along this stretch of road.

The Exchange Vaults
Exchange Street, Cheapside, Wolverhampton, WV1 1TS

The Exchange Vaults used to be a Corn Exchange and was certainly used as such in the 1860s. In the late nineteenth century, the pub had a reputation as a haunt for footpads and highwaymen. Close by there was a now long gone coach house and the story goes that employees of the coach company would supplement their somewhat meagre wages by letting the local criminal elements know when wealthy passengers were travelling.

The haunting of The Exchange Vaults has military connections with both the First and Second World Wars. During the First World War, one Captain Roger Tart, of the South Staffs Regiment, had a favourite seat in the corner of the bar. When he left for the front he told fellow customers to save his place. The unfortunate Captain Tart never returned alive to claim back his corner seat, but his ghost is said to haunt the right hand side of the public bar. Extreme temperature drops are often experienced when the Captain is around.

Andrew Beswick, a sailor in the Second World War, is another spirit said to haunt the Vaults. He had an ill-fated affair with a married woman until her husband found out. According to psychics who have visited the pub, there are a number of restless spirits joining the regular customers!

Odd occurrences often happen in the pub. Lights flicker, beer goes off for no reason, plants refuse to grow, barrels empty themselves and an old photo in the corner by Captain Tart's seat is said to have changed from time to time without any human intervention.

According to staff at the pub the bar stools will sometimes be moved by an unseen force. Down in the cellars electrical problems plague just one particular

The Exchange Vaults.

area. On one occasion while down the cellar on his own Darren, an assistant manager, turned around to be faced with a bizarre sight. Unseen and silently, a bar stool from upstairs had been placed immediately behind him blocking his exit from the cellar. On another occasion Darren was again on his own down the cellar tapping a barrel of bitter at lunch-time, when he clearly heard a little girl's voice call his name. This phenomena has also happened to other staff members as well.

The Greyhound & Punchbowl
High Street, Bilston, WV14 0EP

The Greyhound & Punchbowl is an historic building which is probably older than the High Street on which it stands. Though it has been a pub for more than 200 years, it can trace its history back more than five centuries. Built in the fifteenth century as the Manor House of Stow Heath, it would have originally been surrounded by woodland, a far cry from the bustling main shopping street of today.

Sometime in the nineteenth century, the name 'John Mollesley 1483' was found carved into an old beam in one of the bedrooms. It is quite possible that he built the house, as he was related through marriage to the ancient owners of the manor, the De Bilstons.

Today, this pub still has many genuine surprises for the visitor. There is an elegantly carved sixteenth century mantelpiece, oak panelling and extraordinary but beautiful plaster work. An unusual talking point is the slender, twisted tree-trunk in the centre of the pub. This slender pillar reaches from floor to ceiling and local folklore has it that it marks a medieval drinking place.

Sometime in the eighteenth century, the building became a pub simply called 'The Greyhound'. The 'Punchbowl' part of the name was added a few years later, apparently in recognition of the 'punch bowl ghost' who, legend has it, amused himself by walking from the smoke room to the bar clutching a glass of whisky!

Recent sightings of a ghost in the pub may not be the 'punchbowl ghost', but a rather more sober figure from Bilston's past. The mother to one of the licensees, Doris, would help out in the kitchen on occasions when things got busy. One evening she was sat in the lounge of the pub with the rest of the family. As she glanced out of the window she caught sight of a tall sinister figure walking towards the kitchen, dressed in a long black cloak and wearing a large black hat. Although she was at first startled by this figure, she dismissed it as no one else seemed to have seen him. It was only as she turned her attention back to the conversation that her young daughter said, 'Mom, there is a man going into the kitchen, we had better tell him he can't go in there.' Fearing that there was an intruder in the building they made a thorough search of the kitchen and the rest of the pub, but found no one!

The Greyhound & Punchbowl.

Another curious sighting, and one that deserves to go down in the annals of paranormal research for its unusual nature occurred only a few years ago. A member of staff walked into one of the pub rooms one daytime to discover it was full of customers enjoying a drink, smoking and laughing. This would be nothing unusual in a pub of course, except that the pub was locked and not open for business! The ghostly customers vanished before the eyes of the startled member of staff. Another apparently mundane experience again occurred when the pub was closed. Two men were seen standing in the main corridor talking when they suddenly vanished!

Sounds of a baby crying which may be related to the ghost of a thirty-three-year-old woman seen carrying her six month old child around the pub as she seeks revenge for her murder at the hands of a former landlord many years ago may, or may not be true. Some suggest that poltergeist activity reported in the pub may be related to this sad story. Another macabre story suggests that the skeletal remains of a young child were discovered within the confines of the chimney above the fireplace in the small lounge.

A curious piece of folklore as opposed to a haunting which readers are recommended to seek out is the footprint of Dick Turpin. So the story goes, in the days when the pub was a coaching inn the notorious highwayman was forced to leap from an upstairs window to escape the long arm of the law. His footprint can still be seen where he landed on the ground.

Hog's Head
Stafford Street, Wolverhampton, WV1 1NA

The Hog's Head is a traditional late Victorian hotel and pub. In those days it was known as The Vine. The present pub retains many of the features from this earlier time. Up until the mid 1970s the building was derelict until being rescued and used for insurance offices. In 1997, Hogshead purchased the building and set about returning the public house to its former glory.

More than one ghost haunts this particular hostelry. One story concerns a train driver called Marber. He liked to enjoy a pint or two in between driving trains to and from London in the Second World War during the bombing. Unfortunately, he never returned from one of these hazardous journeys. However, his ghost is said to return to the Hog's Head every now and again seeking the comfort of a quiet pint and convivial company. That old character at the bar may not be quite what he seems.

The pub still has many old customers from years back, some of whom are in their seventies and eighties. The father of one of the older customers owned the hotel in the 1930s. He had a fatal accident when he fell down the cellar steps. His ghost is said to wander the cellars trying in vain to complete the job that was interrupted by his sudden and tragic death. To this day, staff feel very wary of going down into the cellars on their own. Often it feels as though someone is watching them, particularly on the steps where the death took place. Elsewhere in the pub glasses have been known to jump off the shelves for no apparent reason. Keys go missing

Hog's Head.

and then either reappear in bizarre places or else will appear in places previously searched by staff.

The Horse and Jockey
Wood Green Road, Wood Green, Wednesbury , WS10 9AX

The Horse and Jockey is an imposing late Victorian pub with its own large car park. Today, Wood Green is busy with motorway traffic and visitors to the nearby retail park. In Victorian times the area was at the hub of Wednesbury metal manufacturing activity, served by the Grand Junction Railway which arrived at Wood Green in 1837. One feature of the pub which creates a direct link with the past is the unusual ceramic bar counter which has remarkably survived over the years.

According to local legend, the Horse and Jockey was the scene of a tragic suicide. A man walked into the pub, ordered a double brandy, drank it and then promptly shot himself. Whether or not this is the origin of the ghost staff and locals call 'Cyril' is not known, but he certainly makes his presence felt in the pub. On occasions loud banging noises are heard and cold spots felt throughout the bar areas and down the cellar with no obvious causes. On the back stairs the light keeps switching on and off as if by some mischievous hand.

In 1997, Sheila and Rona, two members of staff, were sitting in the lounge bar relaxing when they were suddenly aware of movement noises followed by loud banging coming from the kitchen. Thinking someone may have broken in they went to investigate only to find the kitchen silent and deserted.

However, the activity is by no means restricted to cold spots and banging noises. One morning at around 9.15 a.m., staff member Sheila was on her own in the pub doing some cleaning. The toilet door was banging so she went and moved a stool to prop it open. As she did so the polished spring operated door suddenly flew open and Sheila clearly saw the reflection of a short man in a long overcoat go into the toilet and the door then banged shut. The area around the toilets seems to be particularly active as regulars have reported seeing a similar figure at other times.

The Horse and Jockey.

On occasions a figure is seen on and around the steps leading up to the car park. Recently, a young lady working as a chef watched someone walk down the steps from the car park and fully expected a customer to come in through the door. Needless to say, in keeping with other events at this pub there was nobody there.

The Leopard
Moor Street, West Bromwich

The Leopard was formerly situated in Moor Street, West Bromwich. When new pub licensee Paul Moore took over the pub in 1998, he certainly got more than he bargained for with spirits of another kind!

Alone in the pub one evening, Mr Moore was shocked to see the apparition of a male figure standing by the bar. Before his eyes the ghostly image vanished, once again leaving the stunned licensee alone in the pub.

Local historian Linda Gibbons, who has been researching the pub's 130-year old history, believes she may know who the apparition was. She believes the ghost could be that of the first licensee, Peter Pearson, who originally made his own beer to sell in the pub from 1861.

Former landlord of The Leopard, Harry Smith retired in February 1998, but he is convinced the pub was haunted. He said that he regularly felt a strong presence in the pub, mainly when he was on his own after closing time.

In October 1998, following Mr Moore's sighting the *Black Country Evening Mail* newspaper carried the headline 'Haunted Pub Calls the Ghostbusters'. Parasearch members David Taylor and Ron Lucas were quoted in the article about their intentions for Parasearch to hold a scientific investigation at the pub to see if anything could be recorded on film.

The Little Chop House
Windmill Hill, Colley Gate, B63 2BZ

The Little Chop House nestles beside a busy main road between Lye and Halesowen. Inside is a haven from the noise and traffic of the outside world. But the building has not always been used as a pub. In its 400 year history it has been used, among other things, as an undertakers! The road is named, not surprisingly, after two windmills that stood on the summit of the hill.

When new licensees Mick and his wife Wendy moved into the pub in April 1999, they began to realise that the pub hid a ghostly secret. A strange, unearthly draught blew through the building, doors opened and closed on their own and one of the beds would dip down as if some invisible person was sitting on it. Along with these strange experiences, Mick also heard footsteps in the bar and on occasions his watch would go missing, only to turn up in the most unlikely places.

The Little Chop House.

Stories that the pub is haunted are well known among the staff. Mick's wife Wendy explains: 'We had been told by the cook who has been here for 13 years, that every time new tenants take over the pub the ghost is active.'

The ghostly goings on are said to be caused by the spirit of a young girl who died of scarlet fever in 1903. The room where she died was sealed up and remained so until it was opened a few months after Mick and Wendy moved in as part of extensive refurbishment to the pub. Since the room was opened up and refurbished the strange goings on have ceased, but you never know, they could continue at any time.

The Malt Shovel
Tower Street, Dudley, DY1 1NB

The Malt Shovel is one of Dudley's older pubs and dates back to Georgian times. The pub is a small but very popular hostelry with its own car parking. A listed building, the Malt Shovel lies adjacent to the Green Man entry named after another long gone public house. While visiting the Malt Shovel make sure you take a walk up the entry to have a look at the superb sculpture of a 'Green Man' above the entrance. Green Man figures are often seen peering down from the rafters of churches, but we don't know of another example guarding an entry! While you are there look out for a man who walks into the entry only to promptly disappear. Who he is or why he disappears into the entry is not known but he has been seen by a student returning home from nearby Dudley College.

The Malt Shovel is reputed to be one of the most haunted pubs in Dudley. It has also been witness to its share of tragedy. In 1926, the son of the landlord, a man called Bayliss, was found in his bed hacked to death and decapitated with an axe. His half brother, Joseph Flavel, aged twenty-four at the time, confessed to the grisly murder.

Before entering the pub take a glance at the upstairs windows and you may catch sight of a hazy, floating form known as the Blue Boy. This figure has been witnessed on a number of occasions, but always in the upstairs rooms.

The Malt Shovel.

An apparition of a small adult person has been known to enter the lounge bar, sometimes accompanied by a black dog. Staff have felt invisible hands push them while in the pub's extension. Glasses have also been known to fly off the shelves for no obvious reason seemingly propelled by the same invisible hands.

When we were doing the research for the book Andrew Homer witnessed the glasses hung up behind the bar suddenly start shaking as if something or someone was desperate to make their presence known!

The Manor House
Hall Green Road, Stone Cross, West Bromwich, B71 2EA

The Manor House is without doubt the oldest pub within the pages of this book. It is a priceless example of a medieval timber-framed hall. The earliest surviving part is the hall, which may be assigned on architectural grounds to the late thirteenth or early fourteenth century when the manor of Bromwich was held jointly by the Dudley barony of the Devereux and Marnham families.

The Manor House is a real historical gem. Two of its more unusual features are a moat which it is believed dates from the fourteenth century and a chapel, which dates from the late fifteenth or early sixteenth century. Clay floor tiles discovered in the chapel during restoration are similar to some found in Sandwell Priory, which is hardly surprising as in the Domesday period the manor of Bromwich belonged to William Fitz-Ansculf, the Baron of Dudley, who also had Sandwell Priory built in 1180.

For many years the Manor House faded into obscurity. Known simply as numbers 146 to 160 Hall Green Road, all trace of its ancient past had long ago been hidden by modem bricks and concrete. In 1952, the local council decided that the building (still not regarded as medieval) was beyond repair and should be pulled down. Thanks to the work of a Mr W. Maurice Jones, Architect of Worcester, the building was saved when he discovered its true past and architectural importance. It was estimated that the restoration project would cost £9,000. After several setbacks, the restoration was finally completed in 1960, and soon after this the building was purchased by Ansell's Brewery Ltd.

Since 1995, members of Parasearch have been the only serious scientific group to investigate the strange goings on at the pub. Their first visit with members Chris Wright and David Taylor was a good indication of things to come. Minutes before they arrived, staff in the restaurant had seen an unidentified ghostly figure in the deserted upper Solar Bar.

It wasn't long before Parasearch had returned armed with all their scientific and technical equipment; because the Manor House is so big it was difficult to monitor the entire building. Special attention was therefore focused on the areas where supernatural occurrences had been most often reported. The Great Hall with its stone floor and wooden timbers still gives the Manor House a unique feel. During one investigation Parasearch secretary Carolyn Adey and the treasurer

The Manor House.

Dennis Bache were monitoring the Great Hall. As the investigation drew to a close they both felt the atmosphere change and a foreboding feeling that something was about to happen enveloped both of them.

It was at the exact moment that Dennis turned to get his camera that Carolyn saw the apparition, 'I had a clear view of the whole of the Great Hall as the atmosphere appeared to change. I felt the temperature suddenly fall and the supporting beams began to contract in response to the sudden chill. Suddenly, on the left hand side of the hall I became aware of a figure standing motionless against the wall. A solid figure of a man, aged around thirty-five with shoulder length hair, he appeared to be wearing some sort of white shirt and dark brown waistcoat. He was looking at me, eye to eye. He looked nervous and I got the impression that given the first opportunity he would turn on his heels and run! I could see every detail of the colour of his eyes, texture of his skin, the style of his hair – a real looking person. In fact I thought he was an intruder until I blinked and he vanished instantly!'

Other areas have proved to be equally rewarding. To the left of the main bar is a tiny wood panelled room. It was here that Parasearch member and co-author Andrew Homer was witness to some very strange dancing light effects. No natural explanation for these strange, random lights could be found. Similar lights have also been seen by Parasearch member and professional psychologist Tony Burgess. Former landlord, David, had a scary encounter with a mysterious apparition on the stairs. What made this ghostly encounter so unusual was that the figure was just a glowing red outline, rather like the old Ready Brek advert!

Margaret Webb is a well known local dowser as well as being a member of Parasearch. Using her natural talents she has identified several spirit presences both inside the pub and in the courtyard outside.

Slightly more unusual is the possible ghostly cat that haunts the upper Solar Bar. On one occasion, members of Parasearch were joined by a feline companion – a large black cat. Although it stayed with them for most of the night, no one remembers touching or stroking the cat. It was only afterwards when mentioned to the Manager that it was pointed out that there were no cats in the pub especially as food was prepared on site. They would simply not be allowed. It did emerge later that workmen fitting new carpet in the toilets in the Upper Solar had reported hearing sounds like a cat's claws scratching wood while they had been working. Perhaps this is just another ghostly resident of this atmospheric pub.

The Miners Arms
Ruiton Street, Lower Gornal, DY3 2EG

The Miners Arms is known locally as the 'Chapel House'. This association is due to the use of a room in the pub by the so called 'Gornal Ranters'. These were 'Primitive Methodists' who were prevalent in the Gornal area in the eighteenth century. Their preachers were so fired with enthusiasm that they used to 'rant' at their congregations. The Miners Arms is another pub which came about through the Duke of Wellington's Beerhouse Act of 1830. Home owners were able to pay the sum of two guineas to open their homes to the public for the sale of beer and spirits – hence 'public houses'. The Miners Arms took its name in 1882, and typical of many Black Country pubs was a home brew house. Unusually, the pub cellars were also once used as a jail. There used to be police houses just around the corner and the cellar was a handy and secure place to lock up miscreants!

The Miners Arms has a number of stories associated with it. Approximately fifteen years ago, a previous landlord (known only as John) was sitting on a stool by the bar. A male customer came in and sat on the stool next to him. Nothing particularly unusual in that you may think except that before he could order a drink the figure disappeared into thin air right in front of the astonished landlord. A previous barmaid was also witness to the same figure but this time on the stairs.

A remarkable incident occurred one night about twenty years ago. After an undisturbed night's sleep; the landlord came down in the morning to be greeted by a bizarre sight. All the furniture in the pub had been moved and left scattered around the bar and the lounge. Even stranger, a heavy wooden cabinet at the far end of the pub had been moved all the way to the front door. No other damage was done, nothing was taken and all the doors and windows were still locked. All of this occurred without a single sound being heard from upstairs.

The Miners Arms.

The Noahs Ark
Wood Street, Tipton, DY4 9BQ

The Noahs Ark is a real ale pub situated in a quiet road just yards from the busy Owen Street in Tipton.

Tom Cartwright, an old landlord of the Ark, was once a professional welterweight boxer with some 600 fights to his credit. Tom certainly wasn't afraid of anyone and could certainly look after himself if any trouble broke out, but trouble of a ghostly kind, now that's a different matter.

The Noahs Ark.

One night, Tom was awoken by a figure standing at the foot of the bed. As he lashed out with his deadly fists, the figure just vanished! A few nights later Tom's wife saw the same figure, which she described as 'a young man in his late teens, dressed in a heather mixture tweed suit. He had fair hair and brown eyes. He certainly did not look like a ghost. He had the happiest, most contented look I've ever seen. When he saw me staring at him he just vanished.'

When the Cartwright's described their friendly ghost to regulars in the pub, they were able to accurately identify him as the nineteen-year-old son of a previous landlord who had met a sudden death.

The Old Cat
High Street, Wordsley, DY8 5RT

The Old Cat is the oldest pub in Wordsley. Its unusual 'cottage' exterior betrays the fact that at the turn of the nineteenth century it was originally three cottages. Situated as it is at the very heart of Wordsley, on the main road from Stourbridge to Wolverhampton, makes this a popular pub with both locals and visitors.

Some years ago the Cat, like many pubs in the Black Country, was plagued by a mysterious doodler who left drawings of the Italian Opera singer Mario Lanza

The Old Cat.

sketched in ballpoint pen on beer mats. No one ever owned up to these minor works of art, and they have become part of local folklore.

Another mysterious visitor, although an altogether more ghostly one, is the spectral image of a cavalier occasionally seen in the cellar. On several occasions this historical figure has scared staff working in the cellar changing over barrels. Who he might be is unclear, although local folklore says that King Charles II himself passed through Wordsley after the Battle of Worcester. Could this cavalier be a vestige from the fateful journey of King Charles and his defeated army?

The Old Hop Pole
West Bromwich, High Street, Carters Green, West Bromwich, B70 9LD

The Old Hop Pole is a quaint old Victorian pub situated in the Carters Green area of West Bromwich. The pub stands within sight of the magnificent gothic style clock tower designed by Edward Pincher and built in 1897. The Clock Tower is a symbol of the town's growth and prosperity in Victorian times and is dedicated to one Ruben Farley, the town's first honorary freeman and five times mayor.

The Old Hop Pole has an interesting link with the history of brewing in the area. It still has stained glass panels from the old Showell's Brewery which was founded around Langley and Oldbury in 1887. Showell's brewery is now long gone and was acquired by Samuel Allsop Ltd in 1914. The purchase included some 194 tied houses of which the Old Hop Pole was one.

In common with many of the pubs we investigated for this book the Old Hop Pole boasts strange goings on down in the cellar. Gas keys for the barrels and spanners will often go missing for no apparent reason, but much worse was experienced by an unfortunate previous landlord of the pub. On one occasion he was working away down in the cellar when all of a sudden he was physically lifted right off his feet by an unseen force and thrown across the room. Following this terrifying event the landlord's lower back bore marks where he had been thrown against gas knobs situated high up on the wall.

The ghostly happenings in the Old Hop Pole are by no means limited to the cellar however. There are reports that a little boy has been seen talking to a little girl in Victorian style clothes. The pub features a little snug, which seems to be a centre for paranormal activity. Animals behave strangely in this area. The pub cat has been to known to sit and stare at the corner as if watching some unseen events and dogs seem scared of that particular part of the building. The same corner is prone to inexplicable icy chills even though the rest of the pub is cosily warm.

The Old Hop Pole.

In August 1999, a clue to the possible origin of the haunting was provided by two young female customers. They witnessed the apparition of an old man in a cloth cap sitting in the snug. What the girls did not know, however, was that a previous landlord had died in the snug while in the process of counting out his money.

The Old Priory
New Street, Dudley, DV1 1LT

The Old Priory is named after the Cluniac Priory of St James, which was founded by Gervaise de Paganel between 1160 and 1180.

The figure of a lady is said to haunt the upstairs part of the building at night. Bedroom windows mysteriously open by unseen hands. Two relief managers, staying in the pub overnight, were so disturbed by the sound of someone walking up and down outside their bedroom doors that they ended up spending a fearful night huddled together in one room.

If you visit the pub, watch out for glasses which have been known to fly off a shelf above the bar for no apparent reason. Barrels are regularly heard being moved around in the cellars when there is no-one down there. On more than one

The Old Priory.

occasion staff have been grateful to get away from the pub when the banging is at its worst.

The Old Stags Head
Pennwood Lane, Penn, WV4 5JB

The Old Stags Head is well over 200 years old and holds a commanding view over Penn Common. The Common used to be a popular place for Black Country folk to go out for the day and The Old Stags Head was one of a number of hostelries in the area which provided food and drink to the day trippers. This comfortable, white painted inn is set close to Saint Bartholomew's church. Local legend has it that the cellar of the pub and the church are linked by a passageway, but no sign of this remains today. In 1912, the remains of an Anglo-Saxon stone cross were discovered in the churchyard, said to have been erected by Leofric, Earl of Mercia. Leofric was Lord of the Manor of Upper Penn and his wife was the famous Lady Godiva who rode naked through the streets of Coventry.

If you approach the pub from the Gospel End side look out for a strangely out of place ornamental building on the edge of the common. This building was the site

The Old Stags Head.

of the old Penn Brewery which boasted its own natural spring and ready supply of ingredients for beer making fresh from the local fields. The brewery was never very successful, however, and finally closed down in the early twentieth century.

The haunting of The Old Stags Head combines local legend with strange occurrences in the pub. Legend has it that a vicar of next door St Barts would take advantage of a tunnel connecting the two buildings and frequently nip through for a pint or two between services. His disgruntled wife, so it is said, would follow her husband through the tunnel and regularly turn the beer taps off in disgust.

It is, however, the wife rather than the husband who still seems to frequent the hostelry. For on occasions, the beer taps are found to be turned off when no-one has been down in the cellar. The cellar itself has a disturbing atmosphere at times and pub dogs will never venture down there.

The Landlord's daughter, Louise, once witnessed the apparition of a lady dressed all in black in one of the bedrooms. Over the years there have also been reports of a 'lady in white' who sits in the bar lounge dressed in a Victorian-style gown. She has been seen by both staff and customers at various times over the years. If she is indeed the errant vicar's wife, perhaps she still waits to catch him red handed.

The Olde White Rose
Lichfield Street, Bilston, WV14 0AG

The Olde White Rose dates back to the sixteenth century and is steeped in history and atmosphere. The pub has an extensive network of cellars, some of which are mysteriously bricked up. Until fairly recent times the original stables, complete with fittings, could be glimpsed through the back windows of the greatly extended lounge. Nowadays, the pub has just one extended lounge bar with comfortable seating and tables for meals. A great deal of effort has gone into making The Old White Rose the welcoming hostelry it is today.

When Landlord, John took over The Old White Rose he was told by locals that the pub was haunted. He dismissed the stories as nonsense until early one Thursday morning:

It was winter 1998 and I was getting ready for the usual Thursday morning delivery. Basically, our dray delivery arrives between 7.00am and 7.30am so I get up at about 6.45am to prepare the cellar. I take the empty barrels from the working cellar along to the end of an old disused cellar. There is a 'drop' there where the old barrels can be lifted out and full barrels dropped down into the cellar system. On this particular morning it was about 6.55am by the time I'd got ready. I opened the main door to the disused cellar, put on the light and took a step in. To my surprise I saw a pair of trousers coming down the drop and then the figure came into full view. I realised in that moment that I wasn't looking at an intruder, I was looking at an apparition. He was no more than 10 to 12 feet away and he never flinched. He never moved, he never acknowledged that I was there at all. It was as if he was doing some kind of routine

The Olde White Rose.

and nothing was going to stop him. He had fairly unruly hair, he was a bit swarthy and had very bushy eyebrows. His dress style was far from modern; with very baggy black material trousers and a grey buttoned up tunic top. The clothes looked more well used than scruffy. He appeared to be about middle-aged with very dark hair and pale, gaunt features. He was standing with his head bent down looking at his hands which were palm up. I watched him for what seemed like an age but was probably less than a minute. He then turned and disappeared into a passageway to the left of where he was standing. Actually it is more of an alcove really. The thing is though, the other end is securely bricked up!

The Queen's Head
Level Street, Brierley Hill

The Queen's Head was formerly situated in Level Street, Brierley Hill. One night, sometime in 1977 while the licensee was on holiday, the relief manager and his wife were startled by the sound of men's voices and what sounded like furniture being moved about, coming from the bar. It was after hours, and there shouldn't have been anyone in the pub. Thinking that someone had broken in, they cautiously went downstairs to investigate. What they found was equally as shocking. The pub was empty and secure. Despite the sound of furniture being moved around, nothing had been disturbed!

News of this after-hours activity soon reached the ears of the pub regulars. They claimed that a secret tunnel lay underneath the pub and may at sometime in the past been used as an escape route. This story may or may not be true, as stories of secret tunnels are common local legends. One thing is true however; the licensee's dog would not enter the cellar under any circumstances, as if it could sense some unknown presence lurking in the dark.

The Red Lion
Wombourne, Battlefield Hill, Wombourne, WV5 0JJ

The Red Lion stands on the ancient medieval road linking Wolverhampton with Worcester and Chester. Local legend has it that Battlefield Hill marks the site of the Battle of Tettenhall, but there is scant evidence for this. The ancient white painted inn is entered through a heavy wooden door leading to the bar and comfortable, welcoming lounge.

Wombourne's oldest surviving public house, The Red Lion has been a licensed house from the early nineteenth century, but the building is very much older. Beer used to be brewed on the premises as the Lion had its own well. Long since covered over, the well is situated in the lounge under a square brick pillar by the bar.

The Red Lion is reputedly haunted by the ghost of a lady. When Frank and Lillian (Lil) Ward first moved to the pub in 1963 the ghost made her presence felt by banging doors as she moved through the pub, though she was never seen. Lil was told by locals that the pub was haunted by a previous landlady who they thought had met an untimely death in a fall down the cellar steps.

Things were quiet for many years until a sighting in the early 1980s by Frances, a long serving barmaid. Author Andrew Homer lived nearby at the time and knew the licensee and the staff well. At the time of the sighting, which was early evening, the only people in the lounge were Francis, standing behind the bar, Andrew Homer and his father, Winston Homer. We were just casually chatting with Francis when she was suddenly startled by something happening behind us. She had clearly seen the head and shoulders of a figure pass from right to left through a long rectangular window opposite the bar. At first, I could not understand why this should be unusual until Francis took me outside to view the window. Firstly, the window was down a side entry barred by a stout wooden door which Francis had to unlock. Secondly, the ground below the window was well below the floor of the lounge. The figure would have to have been well over 10 feet tall to pass by the window or of course was walking on a long gone pathway. Francis could

The Red Lion.

not discern any features except to say she was absolutely convinced someone had passed by that window.

In the middle to late 1980s, landlord Lee Thacker took over the Lion and was convinced that the lady ghost was still active. On one occasion while on his own in the pub he caught sight of a lady in Victorian style dress sitting in the lounge area. He only saw her briefly, but following this experience he quickly had the pub blessed by the local clergy. This did not see an end to the sightings however. Around this time a security CCTV camera system was installed in the pub with one camera covering the lounge area. After clearing up one night the staff were relaxing upstairs in the room where the security monitors were set up. Everyone present was amazed to see the white hazy figure of a lady, just as Lee had described, sitting on a seat in the empty and now locked lounge. Lee bravely went down to see if anyone had been locked in the pub by accident, but when he unlocked the door to the lounge there was no more sign of the mysterious lady.

The Shrewsbury Arms
Wolverhampton Street, Dudley, DY1 1DA

The Shrewsbury Arms can trace its history back to 1819, when it was known as the Talbot Hotel. Locally it is known by the curious name of 'The Cow Shed', because it used to be next door to a slaughter house! The pub is situated close to Dudley's medieval marketplace and is integral to the town's character. In the marketplace a touch of Italian flair can be found in the renaissance style drinking fountain designed by James Forsyth in 1867. At the top of the High Street is the distinctive St Thomas' or 'Top Church', one of the first buildings in the world to use iron and timber in the construction of its rafters.

On several occasions a figure in a cloth cap has been seen in both the cellar and the bar. Marlene, who used to work at the pub in the 1980s, saw the figure of an old man in a cap while she was checking the barrels in the cellar. On another occasion the same figure has been seen walking around in the bar when the pub is closed.

Staff have called this benign apparition 'Old Joe' and have speculated that if he is not an old landlord or regular, he may have some connection with the slaughterhouse that used to be next door.

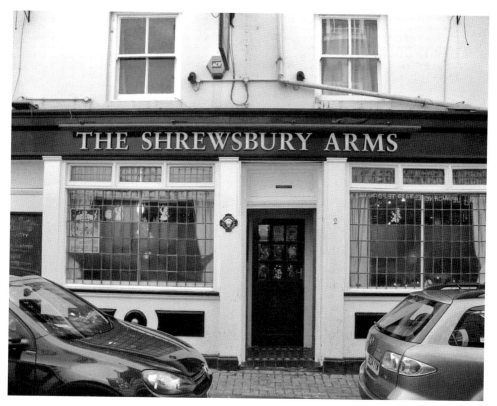

The Shrewsbury Arms.

The Starving Rascal

Brettell Lane, Amblecote, DY8 4BN

The Starving Rascal is a warm and welcoming pub full of local character and charm, there is a very friendly welcome to all. The pub was built about 1850, and originally called 'The Dudley Arms'. In May 1974, its name was changed to 'The Starving Rascal'.

Brettell Lane can be traced back to at least 1774 when it appeared on Robert Whitworth's 'Stourbridge Canal' survey map. Thomas Webb, the famous glass manufacturer at Amblecote in the mid-nineteenth century, called his ironworks the Bretwell Ironworks after an early spelling of the modern Brettell.

The change of name in 1974 was said to commemorate an event in the Victorian history of the pub. So the story goes, a poor old beggar arrived at the pub one cold winter's day begging for food, drink and warmth. He was met with an unsympathetic landlord, who turned him away. The beggar cursed the pub, and he is said to haunt it still.

A Manager of the Rascal, Lorraine, was adamant she didn't believe in ghosts until the events of one night. She recalls, 'It was about 12.30am, all the customers had gone, my husband was in bed and I was down here by myself. I was filling the fridge with cans when I quite clearly felt somebody touch me on my left-hand

The Starving Rascal.

side. I thought it was my husband and I jumped and turned round but there was nobody there.'

Lorraine is not the only person to have strange tales to tell about the place. Kam, a regular at the pub for over 13 years, saw the figure of an old man sitting at the bar. She turned away for a second, but he had gone when she looked back.

Strange happenings also occur elsewhere in the pub. Glasses hanging at the bar swing for no reason and wet footprints appear on the floor, even in dry weather. Lorraine said 'One of the locals, Pete, was standing at the urinals in the gents when the door opened and he felt someone walk in behind him and go into the cubicle. He thought it was one of his friends, so he started talking to him. But he very soon realised that there was nobody there!'

Terry, another regular tells of a more sinister happening, '... the TV above the door flew off its shelf. The bar was absolutely packed, but it hit no-one. There's not really any way it could have fallen by itself.' Pub regular Gary claims to have encountered ghostly goings on in the pub too. Gary says he saw a hand reach out to pick up a pint while he was at the bar; but when he turned round to greet the customer there was no one there!

As with all such stories, there is no evidence that these events actually happened. However, over a period of a few years a group called Parasearch, of which the two authors of this book are prominent members, have been conducting investigations into the reports of ghosts at the pub. Members of Parasearch have been fortunate enough to spend several nights in the building. In the dead of night, when all the regulars have left and everyone is in bed, scientific monitoring equipment has been set up in an attempt to record the pub's spectral residents. Although nothing has as yet been recorded, several Parasearch members have had some very strange experiences.

In the bar, on a few occasions several investigators have reported the movement of a shadowy figure walking around. All attempts to replicate and explain these sightings have failed.

So next time you are standing at the bar waiting to be served, don't be too surprised if you catch sight of a shadowy figure out of the corner of your eye, and make sure he doesn't make a grab for your pint!

The Station Hotel
Castle Hill, Dudley, DY1 4RA

The Station Hotel was originally built in 1910, but the present large hotel dates from 1936. Situated opposite the old Hippodrome Theatre, the Station has played host to many well known celebrities over the years. Famous names who have enjoyed the hospitality of the hotel include Bob Hope, Bing Crosby, George Formby, and Laurel and Hardy.

Beneath the Station Hotel lies a network of old tunnels and cellars which were once witness to a tragic event. Legend has it that 200 years ago a landlord took a young servant girl down into the cellars to supposedly search for a leg of pork.

The Station Hotel.

However, the Landlord had other things on his mind and was determined to have his wicked way with her. The girl would have none of it though and bravely fought back against his unwelcome advances. In a fit of anger the landlord clubbed the ill-fated girl to death and tried to cover up the crime by hiding her body in a vat of ale. To this day staff at the Station Hotel claim to hear the cries of the unfortunate servant girl coming from the cellars on quiet nights.

If you have the nerve to join the Dudley Ghost Walk watch out for an extra 'body' in the cellar. On one of the Ghost Walks, a staff member in charge was startled by a figure brushing past her down the steps into the cellar.

If you decide to stay at The Station Hotel you may find yourself sharing your room with an extra 'guest'. A man described as dressed in black and wearing a pointed hat has regularly been seen by startled guests standing by the bedroom windows in the early hours of the morning.

The Talbot Hotel
High Street, Stourbridge, DY8 1DW

The Talbot Hotel is a Georgian style inn which has a charming tranquillity about it, situated as it is in the busy Stourbridge High Street. There has been a pub on the site since 1685. It was originally called The Brick House, and was the home of the famous Richard Foley (1580-1657), founder of the Foley fortune. He was

The Talbot Hotel.

born in Dudley, becoming its mayor in 1616. He moved to Stourbridge in 1627. It is not surprising that a building of this age has a rich history associated with it. In the late seventeenth century it was used by local religious dissenters as a place for meeting and worship. This was a dangerous time for local dissenters, such as Quakers and Unitarians, as in 1715 a Quaker meeting place in Stourbridge was burnt down. In 1762, The Talbot held the first meeting to enforce the turnpike road between Stourbridge and Colley Gate. The first landlord, Jonathan Pyrke, held cockfighting at the pub, a popular sport at the time. In the 1840s, a theatre was a regular attraction at the Talbot. One of Stourbridge's oldest societies, The Freemasons, have held their Lodge (Talbot Lodge No.119) here since 1733.

Is it any wonder that a pub with such a varied history as The Talbot has a sad and atmospheric ghost story? Sometime in the eighteenth century the landlord at the time had a mistress. She became pregnant by him, but the child was stillborn. The poor child was buried within the walls of the cellar. The mother, the landlord's mistress, died sometime later but how we do not know. Both residents and regulars at The Talbot have reported sightings of a female apparition roaming the building. Is it possible that this is the ghost of the landlord's mistress searching in vain for her long lost child?

The Trumpet
Bilston, WV14 0EP

The Trumpet is a well known pub throughout the Midlands, famed for the wonderful live jazz music it puts on. People come from far and wide to listen to the music, have a drink, and soak up the atmosphere. But if a former barmaid is to be believed, the pub also has a ghostly atmosphere.

The story goes that a barmaid was forced to flee the pub after a series of supernatural experiences which included lights flashing on and off, icy cold spots and unaccountable bumps and bangs. According to the barmaid, the most haunted part of the pub was the cellar, which exuded an oppressive feeling the further one walked into it.

The Unicorn
Bridgnorth Road, Wollaston, DY8 3NX

The Unicorn is a traditional pub nestling at the end of a row of shops not far from Stourbridge ring road. In 1992, it was purchased by a local Black Country brewery, Bathams, who have maintained it as a traditional pub. You won't find any fruit machines, loud music and television here, just a good old-fashioned public house, not too dissimilar to how it may have been in 1859, when it was opened.

And how many pubs can claim a link with the famous Buffalo Bill? In 1904, he brought his famous Wild West Show to Wollaston. He arrived with the 800 performers and 500 horses on three trains at Stourbridge Junction and proceeded through the town to Wollaston. He gave two performances on the 28 April 1904 in a field at Eggington Farm. Today, this is the land between Meridan Avenue and the village side of Bridle Road, where the shops and the Unicorn are now.

The Unicorn is a legendary animal, which supposedly has a horse's body and a single horn projecting from its forehead. The horn is thought to possess magical properties. The association of Unicorns with pubs is always heraldic.

In Lewis Carroll's classic story *Alice Through the Looking Glass*, Alice meets a Unicorn, 'Well, now that we have met', said the Unicorn, 'if you'll believe in me, I'll believe in you. Is that a bargain?' The same could be said for ghosts!

A disquieting occurrence for regulars at The Unicorn, quietly sitting in the pub and minding their own business, is to have their pint of beer tipped into their lap! Rumour has it that the spirit of an old landlord is responsible for this poltergeist type activity. So be careful when you are sitting in this wonderful old pub enjoying your pint. You may want to take a change of clothes with you!

The Unicorn.

Waggon and Horses
Swindon Road, Wall Heath

The Waggon and Horses pub is now long gone. In the later years of its existence it became Christopher's nightclub where Lucy Armstrong provides the following ghostly account:

> This story took place some 30 odd years ago when the father of one of my friends was himself in his 20s. One evening he, as the designated driver, was driving a carload of friends back from an evening out. He was heading towards Kingswinford, along the Swindon road, and had just passed the cross roads that bisect the Mile Flat, also passing the place where "Christopher's" nightclub used to be. As he drove, he became aware of a cyclist going past the opposite way. A car was coming up behind the bike and, as he watched, he saw the car hit the bike and throw it up into the air, along with

the cyclist, and over the roof of the car. He stopped, horrified, demanding to know if anyone else in the car had just seen what he had just seen.

He stopped to look over his shoulder – and could see nothing. There was no car, no bike, no injured cyclist; the road was entirely empty. His friends just laughed at his over-active imagination so he drove on. The incident, and his friends' reaction, really shook him up so he stayed silent about it for years, thinking that no one would believe him. He has never heard of any similar experiences on the same stretch of road and wondered himself at times what on earth it was, but he remains sure of what he saw. Whatever that was ...

The White Rose
Temple Street, Bilston, WV14 0NU

The White Rose was shut down at the time of writing but the building remains, now boarded up. The pub was locally rumoured to be built on the site of a mass grave. In the nineteenth century Cholera epidemics ravaged the population of the Black Country, so while there is no documentary evidence it is quite possible that such a mass grave did exist.

According to locals the White Rose was haunted by a previous landlady, one Lizzie, who on one occasion even appeared on a photograph taken by a local newspaper! A local story has it that Lizzie made a couple of previous landlords leave in something of a hurry. Her apparition appeared to them in the cellar and

The White Rose.

she threw something. Bags were quickly packed and the two left immediately! A previous landlord, Simon, thinks he has heard Lizzie calling his name.

> The first time it happened we had only just moved in. I thought it was someone trying to call me so I went outside, but there was no-one there. I came back in and the voice called again. It was definitely behind the cellar door. I unlocked the cellar and went straight down, but of course there was no-one there.

As with other pubs investigated, everyday items used to disappear only to reappear in obvious places. On one occasion a purse disappeared from the residential part of the pub upstairs. A frantic search proved fruitless but then the purse reappeared on a dresser which had already been thoroughly searched.

Occasionally, the pub was known to play host to a ghostly party in the early hours of the morning. Always at 1.00 a.m. in the morning the sounds of a busy pub would be heard by the landlord and landlady from upstairs. According to Simon, 'The bar sounds full as though there are 25-30 folk in there. You can hear chattering, glasses chinking and a game of pool being played, you come down the first part of the stairs and it all suddenly stops.'

The pub also played host to a shadowy figure who used to walk past the bar door and into the lounge. This figure was seen regularly and was sometimes accompanied by pinpoints of light. However, when staff or customers went to look there was never anyone there.

The Whittington Inn
Stourbridge Road, Kinver, DY7 6NY

The Whittington Inn is situated by the side of the A449 Wolverhampton to Kidderminster road. The large traditional beamed building has a welcoming and homely feel and exudes an atmosphere of history and tradition. The first Whittington Inn was not the present building we see today, but was in fact situated in the nearby Bath Pool Cottages, and was kept by a man named Wynne. It was not until the late nineteenth century that the licence transferred to the present building, which up to then had been the Manor House of the De Whittingtons. The Manor House was built in 1310 by Sir William De Whittington, and it served as a hunting lodge for the royal forest of Kinver. In 1385 Richard Whittington was born, and he went on to become the famous 'Dick Whittington' of fable.

During the Reformation, when many Catholics were being persecuted for their beliefs, The Whittington was used to hide priests, monks and other Catholics in the various priest hiding holes dotted throughout the house. One ingenious hiding place is situated up the chimney in the main bar of the pub – but make sure the fire is out before you have a look!

The building has many links with royalty. It is reputed that Lady Jane Grey stayed here as a child. King Charles II is said to have stayed there after the Battle

The Whittington Inn.

of Worcester. The records report that he, 'Stayed one night at the Manor House of Whittington on the Heath.' Queen Anne also stayed at Whittington in 1711. It was her custom to have her iron seal fixed to the door of the house where she stayed. Amazingly this can still be seen on the main entrance of the present pub to this day – and reads 'Anne R 1711'.

There are four main ghosts associated with the pub. There are vague references to a monk seen by staff and customers. It is believed that he may be the ghost of one of the monks who hid in fear for his life in the building during the Reformation. The other ghost that is likely to give you a fright as you sit quietly enjoying your drink is the figure of a woman in a long flowing dress who is believed to be the ghost of Lady Jane Grey. She has been seen at various locations around the pub, most notably on the stairs in the main bar. There is even a painting of her, by a local artist, pictured as she glides down the stairs. The most recent sighting of the lady in grey occurred a few years ago, when during renovation work Elizabethan wall paintings were uncovered behind wooden panelling in the main bar. Shortly after the paintings were uncovered, the Assistant Manager at the time, Jamie, saw the figure of a woman in a long pale dress walk across the bar towards the staircase and vanish.

Staff who have stayed over at the Inn have also reported strange experiences too. Many years ago a waiter named George, woke up on his third night to feel a presence on his legs and neck. He remained completely paralysed with fear until daylight. The next night, he retired to bed accompanied by the landlord's dog for company. Once again he was woken in the night, this time by the growls of the dog who was behaving as if some invisible force was gripping its neck.

A more recent report comes from Paul, a live-in Chef, who on many occasions woke to find objects in his room had been moved. Other visitors have reported footsteps walking across the landing at night and animals refuse to go into certain areas of the building. Mary, a bar maid at the pub for many years reported a strange case of spontaneous combustion involving a plastic pen, which burst into flame, burning a hole into the wooden surface beneath. The burn mark can still be seen to this day.

You may not have to wait until you get inside to have a ghostly encounter, as the exterior of the pub is also said to be haunted. On the main road directly outside the car park, there have been several sightings off a local notorious highwayman called Captain Kitson. Sightings go back to at least the 1950s and all are similar in content. A figure in tricorn hat is seen on horseback galloping across the fields. In the early 1990s, a nurse returning home during the early hours of the morning had to swerve to avoid hitting the phantom highwayman as he galloped across the main road. So be careful as you drive home!

The other best known ghost associated with the Whittington is the murderer William Howe, although he does not directly haunt the pub. In the eighteenth century, Howe killed in cold blood one Benjamin Robins of nearby Dunsley Hall. Robins was returning from a prosperous day at market in Stourbridge, when he was attacked and left for dead by Howe. The Squire, however, managed to reach help and describe his attacker before he died. Howe was eventually captured and executed for his crime. As a deterrent to the local people of Kinver, his body was gibbeted in a cage in what was then called Fern Tree Hill but later renamed Gibbet Lane. Howe's body disappeared under mysterious circumstances, possibly stolen by a local surgeon who wished to use the body for anatomical experimentation.

It wasn't long before Gibbet Lane gained a reputation for being haunted. A letter to the *Brierley Hill & Stourbridge Advertiser* of December 1872, told of an encounter between a local gentleman and a gliding spectre which loomed up out of the night and vanished as the terrified gent lashed out at it. In recent years courting couples and walkers have reported a variety of experiences in the Lane, including dark shadowy figures and the sound of horses' hooves galloping along the uneven dirt track. Could this be linked to William Howe, or perhaps the macabre skeleton with daggers through its wrists discovered under a tree a few years ago.

The Woodman
Wakelams Fold, Gornal Wood, DY3 2UD

The Woodman is located in the unusually named Wakelams Fold. This area owes its name to the Wakelam family who ran the pub prior to the Second World War. The pub itself is much older and at one time was part of the Earl of Dudley's estates.

Poltergeist type activity is regularly experienced here. Objects are picked up and moved by unseen hands often in full view of astonished staff and customers. The activity is not restricted to the bar area either. Landlord, Alan, recalls the time all the plates in the upstairs kitchen were smashed to the ground all except one which was left intact in the middle of the floor. As recently as Christmas 2009 one of the large main keys to the pub suddenly disappeared. Despite mounting a full search the key could not be found. Not until the following day, that is, when the key reappeared right in the middle of a bed that had been made earlier that same morning.

In the pub itself, staff and customers have learned to expect the unexpected. The television in the bar has been known to turn itself back on. Nothing too unusual in

The Woodman.

that you might think except it often happens after the television has been unplugged from the mains socket for the night. It is always found to have been plugged back in again even though no-one has been anywhere near it.

Serving behind the bar one evening, Alan's daughter witnessed a pint glass float off the bar and gently come to rest again without smashing. Customers too have had full pint glasses lifted off bar tables and even out of their own hands and placed upright on the floor without so much as a drop of beer being spilt! Shortly before obtaining the entry for this book a heavy metal spirit measure was seen by Alan to lift off a shelf behind the bar and hurtle towards the customer he was serving. However, as is typical in much poltergeist type activity, the object fell short of its target and dropped harmlessly to the floor.

Activity at this pub doesn't stop after closing time either. Very often the motion detector of the burglar alarm is set off in the early hours of the morning. Needless to say there are never any human intruders in the pub. However, there are regularly signs that a game of darts has been played in the deserted bar.

Members of local research group, Parasearch, found doors being mysteriously locked and unlocked during an all night investigation at the pub.

So who or what might be responsible for all this ghostly activity? A possible answer may have been given by a visiting psychic who identified two mischievous children and a very stern older gentleman all haunting The Woodman.

The Waggon and Horses
Worcester Street, Stourbridge, DY8 1AT

The trade of most pubs can be affected by a variety of things, most of them economic, and in the case of The Waggon and Horses, supernatural.

In 1860, the licensee, Mr Edward Jones, complained that his trade was being adversely affected by various apparitions on the footpath, known as Gibbet Gullet that ran past his front door. His complaint reached the ears of Lord Lyttleton who set up an enquiry into the matter. Witnesses were produced who testified that three ghosts haunted the lane. Two of the apparitions were of young men who made horrible noises and were naked except for their 'breach clouts'. The third spectre was older and fully clothed except that he was headless!

It was thought that these apparitions were the deceased members of the Walker family. John Walker had been murdered by his two sons, who had in turn been executed at Shrewsbury for their crimes. John Walker's body had been given to a local surgeon for anatomical study, whereas the two sons had been hung from a gibbet probably at the end of the gully outside the pub.

All indications suggest that the pub itself is free from the spectral wonderings of these three apparitions, but just be careful on your way home!

White Hart.

White Hart
Worcester Street, Wolverhampton, WV2 4LQ

The White Hart has a somewhat interesting history. If you thought topless barmaids were a fairly new idea think again as the old Black Country had its own version. However, instead of barmaids it was topless women boxers who used to fight behind this particular pub.

The White Hart is reputed to be haunted by one of the aforementioned topless women boxers. Elizabeth Cartwright was a particularly foul and abusive character who would fight behind the pub for beer slops. Little more is known about her except that her angry ghost is said to throw things around in the pub and push people.

White Lion Inn
Bilston Street, Sedgley, DY3 1JF

The White Lion Inn was being completely refurbished at the time of writing but over the past few years has followed a pattern of opening for just a few months and then suddenly closing again. Whether this has anything to do with the three apparitions said to haunt the White Lion we cannot say, but certainly no-one seems to stay in the pub for very long.

Parts of the white painted building are said to date back to the civil war, with Sedgley forming part of the loyalist stronghold centred on Dudley Castle. This may account for the cavalier who has been seen in various parts of the pub and on the main stairs. Perhaps he had a part to play in the defence of Dudley Castle before it was captured by Parliamentarian forces in 1646.

Staff and customers at the pub regularly witnessed the apparition of an old lady peering into the bar through a small window in the kitchen door. Needless to say no-one, living at least, was in the kitchen when these sightings occurred. She is said by some locals to be the spirit of Ann, the wife of a former licensee. She has also been seen occasionally standing by the fruit machine. In life, Ann enjoyed a glass of gin which may explain why the gin optic is sometimes heard being operated at night but always when the bar is empty.

The White Lion is also home to one of the strangest occurrences we have come across. Throughout this book there are reports of apparitions who, generally speaking, behave as they would have done in life. Indeed, often it is only when a figure passes through a solid object such as a closed door or inexplicably disappears that the onlookers realise they have just witnessed a ghost. However, the third spectre haunting the White Lion seemingly ignores this unwritten rule of ghostly behaviour.

This particular sighting from the White Lion occurs in the main bar area at the front of the building. A man dressed in nondescript attire enters the bar and

White Lion Inn.

White Lion entrance.

approaches the counter as if to order a drink. At this point instead of placing his order the figure is seen by those present to slowly float up off the floor of the bar. He rises up vertically to the ceiling and passes straight through to the function room upstairs. There is no clue as to who this might be or indeed any possible explanation for this strangest of sightings.

Ye Olde Leathern Bottel
Vicarage Road, Wednesbury, WS10 9DW

Ye Olde Leathern Bottel dates back to the sixteenth century and is reputed to be the oldest pub in Wednesbury. Originally a nail maker's cottages, the pub lies on what used to be the old main coach road. It is difficult to imagine now that the quiet side street where the pub resides was once busy with passing horse-drawn trade. A local legend even has it that the pub was once visited by Dick Turpin himself.

Of particular interest for paranormal activity is the little snug at the front of the building. If you look carefully you can see in the corner where a flight of stairs used to be but has been long blocked off. At one time the snug area was part of the vicarage for the local St Barts and was once the vicar's front room. Nowadays, the pub has a great atmosphere and you can be sure of a warm welcome.

There are lots of stories surrounding the Olde Leathern Bottel as befits its great age. Landlord, Derek, reports that he was once down the cellar and heard someone moving about upstairs when the pub should have been empty. Sure enough, when he came up from the cellar to investigate there was no-one there.

A lady in grey is said to haunt the pub and on one occasion a woman in high heels was clearly heard to walk behind the bar, though there was no-one to be seen at the time.

Strange smells are also experienced often in the mornings. A strong smell of toast wafts through the pub regularly even though nobody has used the kitchen or toasted any bread.

The most haunted part of the pub would appear to be the little snug at the front of the building. This was once part of the vicarage of St Barts. The story goes that this part of the pub is haunted by a victim of the 1917 Zeppelin raid. Certain animals will not enter the snug and one of the cleaners refuses to work on her own in the pub. Dave Ogden, local historian and a regular at the pub, maintains that an old man in grey is supposed to haunt the snug and that many women refuse to sit in the corner by the blocked off staircase. Ladies who sit here can expect to experience a sudden temperature drop and a distinct feeling of uneasiness. Try it for yourself if you dare.

Ye Olde Leathern Bottel.

The Yew Tree
Wall Heath

The Yew Tree was formerly situated in Wall Heath. In 1975, Mrs Tibbetts moved into 'The Yew Tree' or 'The Tree' as locals sometimes called it. Nearly a year passed before she and her family began to notice anything strange. During the Christmas of 1976 her family came to stay, and it was then that her son-in-law had an experience he will never forget! While asleep on a mattress in the lounge he was woken up by the sensation that an invisible presence was bearing down upon his chest. He was unable to move and alert his wife who lay asleep next to him. Mrs Tibbett's husband dismissed the experience and any talk of the pub being haunted, that is until he had his own ghostly experience. He awoke early one morning as usual as a delivery of beer was due, and went downstairs to make a cup of tea. As he stood in the kitchen waiting for the kettle to boil, the figure of a woman in a long gown walked past the kitchen door. Thinking it was his wife in her dressing gown he called out to her, but there was no reply. He carried on making the tea, and was surprised when his wife emerged from their bedroom, which was in the opposite direction from which the figure had headed. His wife had clearly only just got up, so who, or what was the figure he had previously seen?

In 1979, the pub underwent modernisation, during which time the most startling ghostly apparition appeared. Mrs Tibbetts walked into the pub to find one of the workmen white with shock. He said that he had been drilling into the wall when all the hairs on the back of his neck stood up. He turned round, and standing behind him was the figure of a tall man, wearing a long, double breasted coat. The workman said that the figure then walked towards the pantry and disappeared. The workman was so shocked and upset by the experience that he refused to set foot back in the pub.

Around the same time Mrs Tibbetts spoke to the previous landlady about an unrelated matter. It wasn't long before the subject of ghosts came up. The former licensee asked if anything 'strange' had happened while she had lived in the pub. She confessed that she had never felt comfortable on her own in the pub and on several occasions the lights had been turned on and off.

Apparitions of a woman in a long gown and a man in a double breasted coat, perhaps we shall never know who, or what, haunted 'The Tree'!

Appendix A

Jack in the Pub!

Out of the dark, supernatural depths of Victorian England one name stands out. Jack. Not Jack the Ripper, but a more supernatural fiend – Spring-Heeled Jack!

It could be argued that he was more notorious than Jack the Ripper, for there were sightings of him outside London. Rumours about Spring-Heeled Jack had swept through the Capital and surrounding villages in the autumn and winter of 1837/38. The figure of Jack was characterised by his ability to leap over high walls, his glowing red eyes, fire breathing and his horns and dark cape. In many respects he is a precursor to the literary Count Dracula, published by Bram Stoker sixty years later in 1897.

Reports of Spring-Heeled Jack soon spread beyond London. In 1845 in Yarmouth, a delirious man wandering about in his nightshirt was mistaken for the fiend and was beaten up. In Peckham in 1872, there was alarm over a ghost leaping over walls and vanishing into thin air with startling speed.

Rumours soon circulated of copy-cat Jacks. In Sheffield in May 1873, rumours sprang up that a tall man in a white sheet was scaring women for a bet. In 1877 at Aldershot barracks, two glowing spectral figures were reported jumping around making a terrible noise by terrified sentries. The last documented reports of Spring-Heeled Jack were in Liverpool in 1904 and Bradford in 1926.

The Black Country did not escape the scare. In 1855, in Old Hill, customers at **The Cross Inn** swore that they saw a frightening figure with cloven hoofs and horns leap from roof to roof straight across the road to the roof of the butchers shop opposite. Police who investigated the sighting confirmed the presence of cloven hoof prints on nearby rooftops. Speculation soon grew that some two legged fiend was roaming the Black Country. Similar reports of hellish hoof prints were apparently frequently reported by quarrymen at Timmins Hill, Dudley and by the landlords of **The Gate Hangs Well** and **The Boat** on Slack Hillock. What makes this story so interesting is that in the same year, cloven hoof prints appeared in the

The mystery of Spring-Heeled Jack.

snow around Devon, leading many to speculate that the Devil himself was stalking the countryside! There were surely those at the time who put the hoof prints down to the demon drink rather than a demon, as many of these reports were close to pubs. For example, reports were made at **The Dragon** (Blackheath), **The Swan** (Whiteheath), **The Wheatsheaf** (Lye Cross) and **The Lion** (Tividale). Rumour soon spread that death followed the hoof prints, and many a superstitious locals must surely have lost much sleep worrying if they were going to be visited next.

Over twenty years later, in 1877, Spring-Heeled Jack put in another equally dramatic appearance along the Himley Road near Wall Heath, not far from the **Dudley Arms** pub. Sentries were posted at several spots along the wooded lane, but they made a hurried retreat after Jack leapt out of the darkness to slap them hard across the face with an icy cold hand before bounding away with his mocking laughter echoing through the night. One Gornal farmer reportedly took a shot at him as he loomed out of the darkness like a monster bat, but the buckshot only appeared to ignite 'a ball of flame from the thing's mouth'. Next morning, a circle of scorched grass in the meadow testified to the farmer's tale. But perhaps Jack lived to tell the tale, for in Dudley in 1882 he jumped out from behind a young courting couple, putting paid to their romantic inclinations!

In Netherton, a terrified old lady was carried into the police station babbling about Spring-Heeled Jack and how she had seen him jump 'across the cut' near Jaw-bone bridge, with flames coming out of his mouth. An immediate investigation was carried out by the local police. As they approached the bridge at midnight they were startled to see a light flying through the air, going from one side of the canal to the other! The brave boys in blue made an arrest, but not of Spring-Heeled Jack! The culprit turned out to be a young Joseph Darby wearing a miner's helmet with lamp attached, as he practiced jumping over the canal! This strange, nocturnal exercise lead Joseph to become the World Spring Jumping Champion, defeating the American holder of the title, W. G. Hamlington, in 1887.

Imitators of Spring-Heeled Jack's antics soon became a national craze. These didn't come any better than the hoax perpetrated by 'Robin Goodfellow' in Birmingham in 1886. In a letter to the local press he announced that he was an acrobat, and he intended to imitate Jack by leaping from the roof of the Market Hall to the spire of St Martin's church in the Bull Ring. On the promised night thousands of people gathered to watch the daring jump, and when Robin/Jack failed to appear, they weren't best pleased!

Warwickshire did not escape the reports of the hellish fiend either. Reports seem to have begun in the region in October 1883, and sometime in 1887 a youth was apprehended as he lay in wait behind churchyard hedges. He was wearing a mask and a white sheet with springs on his feet!

The solution to Spring-Heeled Jack is certainly more prosaic than supernatural. Spring-Heeled Jack fits into a long line of urban scare stories, which have seen their most notable manifestations in *The London Monster* (1788-90); *The Mad Gasser of Matoon* (1930s); *The Halifax Slasher* (1938) and more recently the *Birmingham Vampire* (2005).

Appendix B

Phantom Hitchhiker!

While not strictly associated with any particular pub, nevertheless the following account does owe its origins to a pub trip out from the Black Country and gave coach driver, Stuart Garlick, an experience he will never forget.

It was during a particularly dark night in October 2000 that Stuart found himself driving a group of Black Country revellers to Bridgnorth in Shropshire. Stuart recalls that he saw nothing untoward on that outward journey through the outskirts of Wombourne and out along the Wolverhampton to Bridgnorth road. Rather than park the coach and wait Stuart decided to drive back to Gornal for a coffee in the coach garage and return later for the passengers.

Stuart went back the same way he had come and around 8.30 p.m. he was just passing The Wheel at Worfield. Through the darkness Stuart could see a man in his headlights walking along the side of the road carrying a petrol can. Clearly he had broken down somewhere and Stuart pulled up the coach to offer help. The man gratefully got on the coach and sat at the front in the courier's seat. Although the main internal coach lights were off, Stuart recalls that, 'he was dressed as though he had come straight from a 1960's or 1970's revival night which I thought was rather odd. He had a wide lapel shirt, bell bottomed trousers and an ear length George Best style of haircut. Just the sort of thing you would expect for a 60s or 70s disco night.'

The passenger explained that he had been making his way home from work along the road known locally as the 'rabbit run' and had run out of petrol. He was very grateful that I should stop and give him a lift, remembered Stuart.

We got to the island where you can go straight on for Wolverhampton, turn off left for Telford or turn right for Wombourne. There is a big pub there on the corner. I asked him which way he was going as I was only really killing time and I said I'd drop him off at his car. He did say that the car was off towards Wombourne parked on the

The road of the Phantom Hitchhiker.

verge. I'd got to go that way anyway so we proceeded up towards Tinkers Castle and sure enough, there on the right hand side of the road, on the grass verge was a rather nice looking Triumph TR7 sports car. My passenger said it was a TR8 and that it was pretty rare. I thought it was a TR7 but he was adamant it was a TR8. He also said that the car was a one off and was his absolute pride and joy.

This was right on the crossroads at Tinkers Castle. So I pulled up more or less alongside the car, perhaps a little bit in front. He thanked me for giving him a lift, and said it would have taken him ages to walk back there.

He got off the coach, thanked me again, walked across the windscreen in front of me, waved and disappeared out of sight. Whilst pulling off I then glanced in the offside mirror and he'd gone, completely disappeared! I first thought it might have been a blind spot. With any heavy goods or large vehicle there is a blind spot so I stopped and stuck my head right out of the window bearing in mind I'd only travelled a matter of a couple of yards. The road was straight so there wasn't a curve to obscure my view and he had definitely gone! I couldn't believe it. I looked right out of the window and there was nobody there on that crossroads. It was totally deserted. Not only that but the sports car had completely and silently vanished too!

In the space of about 10 to 15 seconds he had got to get off the coach, walk around the front, cross the road (it was very quiet), open his fuel cap, pour the petrol in, fasten it back, get in his car, turn the engine over to pump the petrol through and then drive off. All of this in about 10 to 15 seconds and with no sound of an engine starting! Well, I can tell you, the hairs on the back of my neck stood on end, I just couldn't believe it. I tried to get away as fast as I could, I was crashing the gears. I just couldn't get away from the area quick enough.

From Stuart's point of view the experience was a real one. He even remembered smelling a whiff of petrol from the can the stranger had. The strange hitchhiker's conversation seemed normal even though his clothes were a little out of date. The only odd aspects Stuart could recall was the fact that the stranger didn't seem to know the area very well and was unclear about how long he had been walking. Stuart is also adamant that had the Triumph been parked there when he had passed by just half an hour before he would have noticed it.

The nearest petrol station for miles around is at Worfield near where Stuart picked up the hitchhiker. Stuart was so bemused by the experience that he contacted the petrol station to see who had been working that night to at least confirm that someone else had seen the mysterious motorist. The manager of the garage explained that because the location is so isolated a decision had been made many years before on safety grounds:

We don't open for petrol here any more at night!

Suggested Further Reading

The Haunted Pub Guide – Guy Lyon Playfair (Harrap, 1985)

Haunted Inns – Marc Alexander (Muller, 1973)

The Haunted Inns of England – Jack Hallam (Wolfe, 1972)

Haunted Inns and Taverns – Andrew Green (Shire, 1995)

Haunted Pubs and Hotels of Worcestershire and its Borders – Anne Bradford (Hunt End Books, 1998)

Gazetteer of British Ghosts – Peter Underwood

Green Men and White Swans: The Folklore of British Pub Names – Jacqueline Simpson (Random House, 2010)

Strangest Pubs in Britain – Strangest Books (2002)

21st Century Ghosts – Jason Karl (New Holland Publishers, 2007)

PARASEARCH

Founded in 1986 to investigate anomalous experiences in the Midlands

Parasearch was founded in 1986 to investigate anomalous phenomena in the Midlands.

Using scientific methods, it has been involved in some high profile investigations of recent years, including the Wem ghost photograph (Shropshire) and Belgrave Hall Museum ghost video (Leicestershire).

Many Parasearch investigations have been featured in the national media, including The Sunday Times, The Daily Express, BBC Television, The Discovery Channel, The Sci-Fi Channel and Living TV.

Parasearch also realises that education is a vital part of what it does, and it has given lectures to various charities and organisations, including the National Trust, the Architecture Centre, Fortean Times UnConvention and the Ghost Club. Parasearch has direct access to expert consultants in various scientific fields including anthropology, psychology, physics and photography.

Parasearch is proud to be an approved regional group for the Association for the Scientific Study of Anomalous Phenomena (ASSAP) and has close links with the Society for Psychical Research (SPR) and The Ghost Club.

Membership of Parasearch is open to anyone with related skills, experience or a strong level of interest to progress in the field of investigation, or who shares its aims of objective scientific methodology to investigate the paranormal.

To report a paranormal experience in confidence, or to apply for membership, visit:

www.parasearch.org.uk

The Association for the Scientific Study of Anomalous Phenomena

ASSAP has been investigating the weird seriously (and the seriously weird) since 1981. Our main aims are paranormal research and education.

We specialise in:

- investigating hauntings and ghost cases
- training paranormal investigators
- researching all anomalous, paranormal and xenonormal phenomena

We publish a newsletter, ASSAP News and a journal, Anomaly. ASSAP is a registered charity in the UK.

www.assap.org